W9-BZW-134

DESCHOOLING OUR LIVES

Edited by Matt Hern

Foreword by Ivan Illich
with Aaron Falbel

NEW SOCIETY PUBLISHERS
Gabriola Island, BC   Philadelphia, PA

Canadian Cataloguing in Publication Data

available from the National Library of Canada

Copyright © 1996 by Matt Hern.
All rights reserved.

Cover design by Kelly Brooks.

Printed in Canada on partially recycled paper by Best Book Manufacturers.

Inquiries regarding requests to reprint all or part of *Deschooling Our Lives* should be addressed to:

New Society Publishers,
P.O. Box 189, Gabriola Island, B.C., Canada V0R 1X0.

Canada ISBN: 1-55092-283-1 (Paperback)
Canada ISBN: 1-55092-282-3 (Hardback)
U.S.A.   ISBN: 0-86571-342-1 (Paperback)
U.S.A.   ISBN: 0-86571-341-3 (Hardback)

To order directly from the publishers, please add $3.00 to the price of the first copy, and $1.00 for each additional copy (plus GST in Canada). Send check or money order to:

New Society Publishers,
P.O. Box 189, Gabriola Island, BC, Canada V0R 1X0

or

4527 Springfield Avenue, Philadelphia, PA U.S.A. 19143

New Society Publishers is a project of the Catalyst Education Society, a nonprofit educational society in Canada, and the New Society Educational Foundation, a nonprofit, tax-exempt public foundation in the U.S. Opinions expressed in this book do not necessarily reflect positions of the Catalyst Education Society nor the New Society Educational Foundation.

Table of Contents

Acknowledgments

There are, of course, an enormous number of people to thank for helping to get this book out, and if I have forgotten to mention any of you here, I apologize sincerely. There is a sea of voices in here, and yours is part of it somewhere.

This book grew out of a magazine, *A Deschooling Reader*, that was funded by the Threshold Foundation. The magazine was successful in large part due to the fine production of Paula, and was only possible, like many things in my life of late, with Sam's generosity.

This collection brings together friends and colleagues, and I thank all the contributors for their efforts, their patience in dealing with my rambling phone calls, my occasionally muddled directives and my tight schedule. These writers have offered up visions that are compelling and genuine, and their lives and work touch far more people than they may realize.

The production of this anthology has been remarkably easy, thanks in large part to the folks at New Society, especially Judith and Kip, who have been unfailingly supportive. Thanks also to Stu Chaulk who has helped immeasurably with getting actual words on actual paper.

There are more. First, everybody at our center. The community of people around our learning center is what informs and sustains me every day, and I thank all the kids and parents for who they are: they make words make sense to me. For artwork and photos, I especially thank Daniel Aarons, Anne Franklin, Val Franklin and Sam Roddick. Second, everybody at Wondertree, especially Maureen and Brent. Third, my folks, Adi and Pa, and a crew of friends in Vancouver who put up with me, especially Stu and Marcus. Also, those people who keep my eyes open late at night and inspire me, even though they don't know it: Ivan Illich, John Holt, Michael Franti, Ani di Franco, Dennis Rodman, Lyle Lovett, Steve Earle, the Beastie Boys, Hal Hartley, Scottie Pippen, Guy Clark, Arrested Development, Michelle Shocked, John Gatto, Shawn Kemp, Murray Bookchin, Mary Leue, and many more.

Finally, for permission to reprint extracts from previously published works, I thank the University of Chicago Press for the pieces *On Education*, by Leo Tolstoy, edited by Weiner; and Harcourt, Brace, & Company for *Family Matters: Why Homeschooling Makes Sense*, by David Guterson (pp. 23-28).

This book is dedicated to Sadie and Selena:
they make it all matter to me.

Foreword

Ivan Illich

L EAFING THROUGH THE PAGES OF *DESCHOOLING OUR LIVES*
transports me back to the year 1970 when, together with
Everett Reimer at the Center for Intercultural Documentation
(CIDOC) in Cuernavaca, I gathered together some of the
thoughtful critics of education (Paulo Freire, John Holt, Paul
Goodman, Jonathan Kozol, Joel Spring, George Dennison, and
others) to address the futility of schooling—not only in Latin
America, which was already obvious, but also in the so-called
developed, industrialized world.

On Wednesday mornings during the spring and summer of that
year, I distributed drafts of essays that eventually became chapters
of my book, *Deschooling Society*. Looking back over a quarter
century, many of the views and criticisms that seemed so radical
back in 1970 today seem rather naive. While my criticisms of
schooling in that book may have helped some people reflect on the
unwanted social side effects of *that* institution—and perhaps
pursue meaningful alternatives to it—I now realize that I was
largely barking up the wrong tree. To understand why I feel this
way and to get a glimpse of where I am today, I invite readers to
accompany me on the journey I took after *Deschooling Society*.

My travelogue begins twenty-five years ago when *Deschooling
Society* was about to appear. During the nine months the
manuscript was at the publishers, I grew more and more
dissatisfied with the text, which, by the way, did not argue for the
elimination of schools. This misapprehension I owe to Cass
Canfield Sr., Harper's president, who named the book and in so
doing misrepresented my thoughts. The book advocates the
disestablishment of schools, in the sense in which the Church has

been disestablished in the United States. By disestablishment, I meant, first, not paying public monies and, second, not granting any special social privileges to either church- or school-goers. (I even suggested that instead of financing schools, we should go further than we went with religion and have schools pay taxes, so that schooling would become a luxury object and be recognized as such.)

I called for the disestablishment of schools for the sake of improving education and here, I noticed, lay my mistake. Much more important than the disestablishment of schools, I began to see, was the reversal of those trends that make of education a pressing need rather than a gift of gratuitous leisure. I began to fear that the disestablishment of the educational church would lead to a fanatical revival of many forms of degraded, all-encompassing education, making the world into a universal classroom, a global schoolhouse. The more important question became, "Why do so many people—even ardent critics of schooling—become addicted to education, as to a drug?"

Norman Cousins published my own recantation in the Saturday Review during the very week *Deschooling Society* came out. In it I argued that the alternative to schooling was not some other type of educational agency, or the design of educational opportunities in every aspect of life, but a society which fosters a different attitude of people toward tools. I expanded and generalized this argument in my next book, *Tools for Conviviality*.

Largely through the help of my friend and colleague Wolfgang Sachs, I came to see that the educational function was already emigrating from the schools and that, increasingly, other forms of compulsory learning would be instituted in modern society. It would become compulsory not by law, but by other tricks such as making people believe that they are learning something from TV, or compelling people to attend in-service training, or getting people to pay huge amounts of money in order to be taught how to have better sex, how to be more sensitive, how to know more about the vitamins they need, how to play games, and so on. This talk of "lifelong learning" and "learning needs" has thoroughly polluted society, and not just schools, with the stench of education.

Then came the third stage, in the late seventies and early eighties, when my curiosity and reflections focused on the historical circumstances under which the very idea of educational needs can arise. When I wrote *Deschooling Society*, the social effects, and not the historical substance of education, were still at the core of my interest. I had questioned schooling as a desirable means, but I had not questioned education as a desirable end. I still accepted that, fundamentallly, educational needs of some kind were an historical given of human nature. I no longer accept this today.

As I refocused my attention from schooling to education, from the process toward its orientation, I came to understand education as learning *when it takes place under the assumption of scarcity in the means which produce it*. The "need" for education from this perspective appears as a result of societal beliefs and arrangements which make the means for so-called socialization scarce. And, from this same perspective, I began to notice that educational rituals reflected, reinforced, and actually created belief in the value of learning pursued under conditions of scarcity. Such beliefs, arrangements, and rituals, I came to see, could easily survive and thrive under the rubricks of deschooooling, free schooling, or homeschooling (which, for the most part, are limited to the commendable rejection of authoritarian methods).

What does scarcity have to do with education? If the means for learning (in general) are abundant, rather than scarce, then education never arises—one does not need to make special arrangements for "learning." If, on the other hand, the means for learning are in scarce supply, or are assumed to be scarce, then educational arrangements crop up to "ensure" that certain important knowledge, ideas, skills, attitudes, etc., are "transmitted." Education then becomes an economic commodity, which one consumes, or, to use common language, which one "gets." Scarcity emerges both from our perceptions, which are massaged by education professionals who are in the business of imputing educational needs, and from actual societal arrange-ments that make access to tools and to skilled, knowledgeable people hard to come by—that is, scarce.

If there were one thing I could wish for the readers (and some of the writers) of *Deschooling Our Lives*, it would be this: If people are seriously to think about deschooling their lives, and not just escape from the corrosive effects of compulsory schooling, they could do no better than to develop the habit of setting a mental question mark beside all discourse on young people's "educational needs" or "learning needs," or about their need for a "preparation for life." I would like them to reflect on the historicity of these very ideas. Such reflection would take the new crop of deschoolers a step further from where the younger and somewhat naive Ivan was situated, back when talk of "deschooling" was born.

Bremen, Germany
Summer 1995

1

Kids, Community, and Self-Design: An Introduction

Matt Hern

THE ABJECT FAILURE OF MONOPOLY, STATE-CONTROLLED, COMPULSORY schooling is evident to anyone who looks. The nightmare of schooling is costing our kids, our families, and communities dearly in every way. Schools waste more money than anyone can fully conceive, demand that our kids spend twelve (twelve!) years of their natural youth in often morbidly depressing and oppressive environments, and pour the energies of thousands upon thousands of eager teachers into demeaning and senseless classroom situations. Government schooling is the explicit attempt to coerce people into accepting their appropriate place in hierarchical, industrial capitalism.

The sanctity of public schools has become so reified in our bizarre North American public political consciousness that people reflexively mouth support for "education spending" or "school dollars" without carefully considering what they are talking about. Behind the sordid liberal-conservative debate about how much cash to allocate to public schools is a system that nurtures the worst in humanity and simultaneously suppresses individuality and real community. And the debate drones on and on regarding how best to prop up this bloated corpse. The reality is that there are much better answers out there—answers that don't require professionals or large amounts of money to make them work.

Opposition to public schooling is being manifested in a plethora of ways, the most compelling of which are those explicitly and entirely rejecting schools and schooling as a construct. The numbers and kinds of homelearners and free schools and learning centers are really staggering. What it means to grow up fully and healthily can be interpreted in an infinite number of ways and, appropriately, there are a near-infinite number of existing interpretations.

There is an important set of distinctions I want to make here. This is a book about deschooling: a series of pieces about what happens when people reject schools. There are a variety of perspectives on schooling in the book, however, and it is critical to separate schools and schooling. Schools practise a certain brand of schooling: they have their own individual ideologies and pedagogical approaches, but they are institutions devoted to schooling, or imparting a certain set of values, beliefs and practices upon their clients. Schooling has found its ultimate (thus far) expression in the current state-run, compulsory, child-warehousing system we call public schools. But schooling can still take place outside schools themselves, and clearly that is what many homeschooling families do: they are *schooling* their kids at home.

All the pieces in this collection share a common opposition to compulsory state-schools, but the authors represent a spectrum of opinion, often very subtly different, on schooling. I consider these differences to be complementary and a strength of the book. The variety of approaches offers a broad perspective and should assist readers in understanding the particular tensions and interpretations within deschooling. This wide vantage point is intended to serve as a map and a guide for developing an informed and individual view of deschooling. I have a very particular personal interest in advocating a rejection of schools and schooling, and in challenging conventional definitions of education and learning as well. I want to draw your attention to these distinctions, and make a brief case here for a full examination of our understanding of what it means to grow as a healthy human being.

★

I have organized the book into four sections, each of which

addresses a specific aspect of deschooling. The book's structure is intended to flow from older philosophical work, to writing from the nineties, to perspectives on homelearning, to pieces on 'unschools.' This progression seems useful to me, in large part as it mimics the path my own thinking took after picking up books by Illich years ago. It is also important to recognize and acknowledge the historical roots of deschooling, and the ways in which opposition to state-schooling has developed over the years. As Illich, John Gatto, and others have suggested, there have been times in the past when neither schooling nor education was considered a requisite for healthy living, and it is critical to understand the political and social circumstances that have subsequently given rise to schools and schooling.

This book is largely about kids. Deschooling, however, is not only about children; it is about people, individuals, families, and communities taking control of the direction and shape of their lives. While the particulars vary, there are several key attitudes that bind these articles together, including, among others: the belief that children are an active, important part of the community; the desire to view the family as an autonomous, self-defining unit; the ability of individuals to focus on their own unique interests; the need to allow people to develop on their own time schedules; and the characterization of deschooling and homelearning as a fundamentally cooperative social project.

These are common themes that surface repeatedly here, whether in the writing of an aristocratic 19th century novelist in Russia or of an African-American homeschooling mother of three in the Pacific Northwest. Opposition to state-schooling is fundamentally a political act, and the defining characteristics of thinking about deschooling focus on the sanctity of individual freedom and, simultaneously, on the essential role of the community in child-rearing.

Currently, more and more voices are joining the dialogue about deschooling, as the entire system of public schooling becomes increasingly difficult to maintain. The failure of compulsory schooling—morally, educationally, economically, physically, and spiritually—becomes more obvious every day, and homeschoolers and deschoolers are being joined by advocates for charter schools, public alternative schools, voucher systems, and much else. The most compelling and viable options are being proposed by those who reject state control and monitoring of children completely, and support the ability of kids, families, and communities to shape themselves. In this collection, there are a variety of viewpoints on deschooling, drawn together by the shared vision of community and self-reliance.

★

The fundamental concept that informs my idea of what is "good" is that of self-design. I believe it is a worthy and honorable goal for every human to be genuinely able to design themselves—to self-manage, self-direct, and self-evaluate their own lives. This means people, including kids, living their lives according to their own peculiar and unique sensibilities, becoming who they want to be.

Schooling and education are antithetical to an ethic of self-design. Schooling is about imprinting values onto people—taking a particular set of values, an explicit view of the way things are or ought to be, and training students to repeat that information in specific ways. The success of schooling can be evaluated in very quantifiable ways. Teaching is the practice of that transfer of information. Teachers are professionals, trained in a variety of ways to coerce, cajole, plead, beg, drive, manipulate, or encourage their students to receive, accept, and repeat the information they are offering.

The teaching profession often attempts to paint its work as "sharing," but the practice of teaching and the act of sharing are very different. The first is a service, in which one person, usually unrequested, impresses a piece of information upon another person, defining what is right and evaluating the other regarding his or her ability to accept and repeat that view. Sharing is about offering one's understanding freely, allowing another access to one's viewpoint, for the other to use as he or she sees fit. One is a supportive relationship, the other is professionalized manipulation.

The term education provides the larger context of schooling. It gives a broad definition of what is good, of what every person ought to know to become a legitimate member of society: it is about shaping another person. Education is not a process that supports self-definition. It is precisely intent upon the opposite: the design of others.

Finally, I want to touch on the idea of learning itself. I hear the word constantly. "Are they learning?" — "What are they learning?" — "What did you learn?" — "I could really learn something there." — "It was a real learning experience...." I comprehend what people intend, but I am unable to conceive of a situation where learning does not take place. I am unable to see where it is possible to separate learning from experience. Learning takes place constantly: we learn when we are asleep, content, daydreaming, bored, angry, rapturous, and every other time, too.

The word learning is employed so often and so loosely because it is a useful code word for defining what is good. Many people use the word to mean that a person or student is behaving or thinking as the teacher wants, that the teaching is "getting through." When people mouthe words that we agree with, or do something we approve of, then they are "learning." Outside of this usage, I can see no real reason to distinguish between learning and living. It is impossible to exist, to experience the world, without learning, so rather than reifying learning as an ideal state, I propose that a worthy goal be self-definition: the practice of self-design through an active, participatory, exciting, fun, diverse, and unique exploration of the world and our lives.

At any age, each individual is best able to define her or his own interests, needs, and desires. Schools assume that kids need to be taught what is good, what is important to understand. I refuse to accept this. Kids do not need to be taught. Our children should be supported to develop and grow into the unique, enigmatic, contradictory individuals that human beings are.

We should nourish the diversity and the uniqueness in all our kids. Parents and families need to surround kids with love and support, not arbitrary authority and petty bureaucracy. I want to encourage adults to *live* with the kids around them, not to service them, and to be in real relationships with them. To go places with kids, to read, to play, to draw with them, to travel with them, to live full lives with them. Our kids do not need us to be professional parents; they need healthy, caring people to use as models, and parents who will support them growing into themselves.

★

There is a myth that deschooling is available only to the privileged. This is simply not true. I know dozens and dozens of unschoolers and homelearners who come from every imaginable sector of society. Refusing schools is a real possibility for everyone, which in no way limits a person's options for the future. It is possible not to go to school and still go to any university, any college, any training institution, to get any job and to go anywhere. It has been my experience, in fact, that unschoolers tend to be more confident, more motivated, and better able to make solid personal decisions than those who have been schooled for most of their natural childhood.

Deschooling does not insulate people from the world: it engages them, demands that they make decisions and participate genuinely in the community rather than waste time in institutions that have logic and meaning only internally. I believe that schooling is a destructive force across the board, its implicit and explicit effect being to further entrench and reinforce society's pervasive hierarchy and inequality. The process has a corrosive effect on everyone involved.

That said, I want to encourage deschoolers at every level to take the analyses and impulses that led them to reject traditional schools and apply them to the wider community. I want people to look at hospitals and cities and eating and houses and sex and city halls and shopping malls and community centers and everything else with the same critical eye they bring to bear upon school. In this context, deschooling plays a critical part in the reconstruction of our communities into more democratic, equitable, just, and participatory enterprises. To paraphrase John Holt, "Imagine your ideal world, and imagine how people would act in it. Now start acting that way right now." Deschooling can and ought to be a huge step towards remaking our communities the way we want them.

★

I want to stress that these are my own particular views, and while they may appear very different from others in this collection, I consider that to be completely appropriate. Often intellectual differences are magnified on paper, while in real life it is the complementarity of practices which becomes evident. While genuine differences between writers exist, I am moved by the practice of the people included here, and of so many others like them who are refusing to be schooled without their consent and who are living their lives with compassion and dignity.

Without schools, the potential of people and communities is enormous. It is the quality of living and of continuing vision demonstrated by the contributors here that make this collection so important to me, and I urge you to hear their voices.

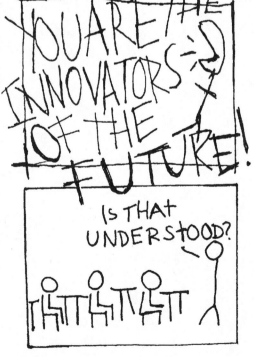

Daniel Aarons

Part One — Looking Back: Some of the Roots of Modern Deschooling

2

On Education

Leo Tolstoy

Leo Tolstoy was born into Russian aristocracy, joined the army and fought in the Crimean War, then founded a school at his estate at Yasnaya Polyana. He wrote prolifically: plays, novels, novellas, treatises, and letters, including Anna Karenina, War and Peace, The Death of Ivan Illyich *and* Resurrection. *His writings on education, nonviolence, anarchism, asceticism, and spirituality found a worldwide audience, deeply influencing Gandhi and Martin Luther King among millions of others.*

This article is a conglomeration of excerpts from various essays Tolstoy wrote in the 1860s in the periodical he published called Yasnaya Polyana, *named after, and based on his experiences at the school on his estate. Tolstoy's thinking is unrelentingly honest, as he rigorously applies his Christian, anarchist, nonviolent, and communitarian ideals to his daily relations with the children. Although more than a century old, his writing still sheds much light on current educational theory and clearly anticipates much of the work of A. S. Neill and the free school movement.*

On popular education

SCHOOL JUSTLY PRESENTS ITSELF TO THE CHILD'S MIND AS AN establishment where he is taught that which nobody understands; where he is generally compelled to speak not his native *patois, Mundart,* but a foreign language; where the teacher for the greater part sees in his pupils his natural enemies, who, out of their own malice and that of their parents, do not wish to learn that which he has learned; and where the pupils, on their side, look upon their teacher as their enemy, who only out of personal spite compels them to learn such difficult things. In such an situation they are obliged to pass six years and about six hours every day.

What the results must be, we again see from what they really are, not according to the reports, but from actual facts.

In Germany, nine-tenths of the school population take away from school a mechanical knowledge of reading and writing, and such a strong loathing for the paths of science traversed by them that they never again take a book into their hands.

It is enough to look at one and the same child at home, in the street, or at school: now you see a vivacious, curious child, with a smile in his eyes and on his lips, seeking instruction in everything, as he would seek pleasure, clearly, and frequently strongly expressing his thoughts in his own words; now again you see a worn out, retiring being, with an expression of fatigue, terror, and *ennui*, repeating with the lips only strange words in a strange language,—a being whose soul has, like a snail, retreated into its house. It is enough to look at these two conditions in order to decide which of the two is more advantageous for the child's development.

That strange psychological condition which I will call the scholastic condition of the soul, and which all of us, unfortunately, know too well, consists in that all the higher faculties, imagination, creativeness, inventiveness, give way to other, semi-animal faculties, which consist in pronouncing sounds independently from any concept, in counting numbers in succession, 1, 2, 3, 4, 5, in perceiving words, without allowing imagination to substitute images for these sounds, in short, in developing a faculty for crushing all higher faculties, so that only those might be evolved which coincide with the scholastic condition of fear, and of straining memory and attention.

Every pupil is so long an anomaly at school as he has not fallen into the rut of this semi-animal condition. The moment a child has reached that state and has lost all his independence and originality, the moment there appear in him various symptoms of disease—hypocrisy, aimless lying, dullness, and so forth—he no longer is an anomaly: he has fallen into the rut, and the teacher begins to be satisfied with him. Then there happens those by no means accidental and frequently repeated phenomena, that the dullest boy becomes the best pupil, and the most intelligent the worst. It seems to me that this fact is sufficiently significant to make people think and try to explain it. It seems to me that one such fact serves as a palpable proof of the fallacy of the principle of compulsory education.

More than that. Besides this negative injury, which consists in removing the children from the unconscious education which they receive at home, at work, in the street, the schools are physically injurious—for the body, which at this early age is inseparable from the soul. This injury is especially important on account of the monotony of the scholastic education, even if it were good. For the agriculturist it is impossible to substitute anything for those conditions of labor, life in the field, conversation of elders, and so forth, which surround him; even so it is with the artisan and, in general, with the inhabitant of the city. Not by accident, but designedly, has Nature surrounded the agriculturist with rustic conditions, and the city dweller with urban conditions. These conditions are most highly instructive, and only in them can each develop. And yet, school lays down as the first condition of education the alienation from these conditions.

More than that. School is not satisfied with tearing the child away from life for six hours a day, during the best years of the child—it wants to tear three-year-old children away from the influence of their mothers. They have invented institutions (*Kleinkinderbewahranstalt*, infant schools, *salles d'asile*) of which we shall have occasion to speak more in detail. All that is lacking now is the invention of a steam engine to take the place of wet nurses.

The school at Yasnaya Polyana

. . . In the village, people rise with the fires. From the school the fires have long been observed in the windows, and half an hour after the ringing of the bell there appear, in the mist, in the rain, or in the oblique rays of the autumnal sun, dark figures, by twos, by threes, or singly, on the mounds (the village is separated from the school by a ravine). The herding feeling has long disappeared in the pupils. A pupil no longer has the need of waiting and shouting: "O boys, let's to school! She has begun." He knows by this time that "school" is neuter, and he knows a few other things, and, strange to say, for that very reason has no longer any need of a crowd. When the time comes to go, he goes. It seems to me that the personalities are becoming more independent, their characters more sharply defined, with every day. I have never noticed the pupils playing on their way, unless it be a very young child, or a new pupil, who had begun his instruction in some other school. The children bring nothing with them, neither books, nor copybooks. No lessons are given for home.

Not only do they carry nothing in their hands, but they have nothing to carry even in their heads. They are not obliged to remember any lesson—nothing that they were doing the day before. They are not vexed by the thought of the impending lesson. They bring with them nothing but their impressionable natures and their convictions that today it will be as jolly in school as it was yesterday. They do not think of their classes until they have begun.

All the pupils meet together for the class of religion, which is the only regular class we have, because the teacher lives two *versts* away and comes only twice a week; they also meet together for the drawing class. Before those classes there is animation, fighting, shouting, and the most pronounced external disorder: some drag the benches from one room into another; some fight; some of the children of the manorial servants run home for some bread, which they roast in the stove; one is taking something away from a boy; another is doing some gymnastics, and, just as in the disorder of the morning, it is much easier to allow them to quiet themselves and resume their natural order than forcibly to settle them. With the present spirit of the school it would be physically impossible to stop them. The louder the teacher calls—this has actually happened—the louder they shout: his loud voice only excites them. If you stop them, or if you can not do that, if you carry them away into another direction, this small sea begins to billow less and less until it finally grows calm. In the majority of cases there is no need to say anything. The drawing class, everybody's favorite class, is at noon when, after three hours' work, the children are beginning to be hungry, and the benches and tables have to be taken from one room to another, and there is a terrible hubbub; and yet, in spite of it, the moment the teacher is ready, the pupils are, too, and if one of them should keep them back from starting, he gets his punishment meted out to him by the children themselves.

I must explain myself. In presenting a description of the

Yásnaya Polyána school, I do not mean to offer a model of what is needed and is good for a school, but simply to furnish an actual description of the school. I presume that such descriptions may have their use. If I shall succeed in the following numbers in presenting a clear account of the evolution of the school, it will become intelligible to the reader what it is that has led to the formation of the present character of the school, why I regard such an order as good, and why it would be absolutely impossible for me to change it, even if I wanted.

The school has evolved freely from the principles introduced into it by teacher and pupils. In spite of the preponderating influence of the teacher, the pupil has always the right not to come to school, or, having come, not to listen to the teacher. The teacher has had the right not to admit a pupil, and has had the possibility of bringing to bear all the force of his influence on the majority of pupils, on the society, always composed of the school children.

★

I am convinced that the school ought not to interfere in that part of the education which belongs to the family; that the school has no right and ought not to reward and punish; that the best police and administration of a school consist in giving full liberty to the pupils to study and settle their disputes as they know best. I am convinced of it, and yet, in spite of it, the old habits of the educational schools are so strong in us that we frequently depart from that rule in the Yásnaya Polyána school. . . .

Education and culture

. . . Culture in general is to be understood as the consequence of all those influences which life exerts on man. . . . Education is the action of one man upon another for the purpose of making the person under education acquire certain moral habits. . . . Instruction is the transmission of one man's information to another (one may instruct in the game of chess, in history, in the shoemaker's art). Teaching, a shade of instruction, is the action of one man upon another for the purpose of making the pupil acquire certain physical habits (one teaches how to sing, do carpentry, dance, row, declaim). Instruction and teaching are the means of culture, when they are free, and means of education, when the teaching is forced upon the pupil, and when the instruction is exclusive, that is, when only those subjects are taught which the educator regards as necessary. The truth presents itself clearly and instinctively to everybody. However much we may try to weld what is disconnected, and to subdivide what is inseparable, and to subordinate thought to the existing order of things—truth is apparent.

Education is a compulsory, forcible action of one person upon another for the purpose of forming a man such as will appear to us to be good; but culture is the free relation of people, having for its basis the need of one man to acquire knowledge, and of the other to impart that which he has acquired. Instruction, *Unterricht*, is a means of both culture and education. The difference between education and culture lies only in the compulsion, which education deems itself in the right to exert. Education is culture under restraint. Culture is free.

★

I spoke in my first article on the right of compulsion in matters of education and have endeavored to prove that, firstly, compulsion is impossible; secondly, that it brings no results or only sad results; thirdly, that compulsion can have no other basis but arbitrary will. ...Education as a subject of science does not exist. Education is the tendency toward moral despotism raised to a principle. Education is, I shall not say an expression of the bad side of human nature, but a phenomenon which proves the undeveloped condition of human thought, and therefore, it cannot be put at the base of intelligent human activity—of science.

Education is the tendency of one man to make another just like himself. (The tendency of a poor man to take the wealth away from the rich man, the feeling of envy in an old man at the sight of fresh and vigorous youth—the feeling of envy, raised to a principle and theory). I am convinced that the educator undertakes with such zeal the education of the child, because at the base of this tendency lies his envy of the child's purity, and his desire to make him like himself, that is, to spoil him.

3

The Intimate and the Ultimate

Vinoba Bhave

Vinoba Bhave was born in the Indian state of Maharashtra in 1895, to Brahman parents. Bhave founded the Bhoodan Yajna or land-gift movement in 1951, and walked to all corners of India, collecting gifts of five million acres of land which he distributed to the poor. Gandhi identified Bhave as his spiritual successor.

This selection of pieces, drawn from a larger collection of work by Bhave, is included because it offers a clear analysis of Western schooling ideals and a powerful vision of self-reliance and children working within community. Satish Kumar (see Chapter 23) describes Bhave as a great influence on him and the Small School movement in Europe.

Self-reliance

MANY PEOPLE WOULD AGREE ABOUT THE IMPORTANCE OF SELF-reliance in education. Self-reliance has a very profound meaning. There must be economic self-reliance through manual labor. Everyone must learn to use his hands. If the whole population were to take up some kind of handicraft, it would bring all sorts of benefits; class divisions would be overcome, production would rise, prosperity and health would improve. So that, at the very least, this measure of self-sufficiency must form part of our educational program.

Education must be of such a quality that it will train students in intellectual self-reliance and make them independent thinkers. If this were to become the chief aim of learning, the whole process of learning would be transformed. The present school syllabus contains a multiplicity of languages and subjects, and the student feels that in every one of these he needs the teacher's help for years together. But a student should be so taught that he is capable of going forward and acquiring knowledge for himself. There is an infinite sum of knowledge in the world, and each one needs some finite portion of it for the conduct of his affairs. But it is a mistake to think that this life-knowledge can only be had in any school. Life-knowledge can only be had from life. The task of the school is to awaken in its pupils the wish to learn from life.

Most parents are anxious for their children to complete the school course so that they can get a salaried job and lead an easy life. This is the wrong way to look at education. Learning has value in its own right. The purpose of learning is freedom. Freedom implies not only independence of other people but also independence of one's own moods and impulses. The man who is a slave to his senses and cannot keep his impulses under control is neither free nor self-sufficient.

The goal of education must be freedom from fear. In the *Upanishads*, when the guru is teaching his disciples he says to them: "O my students, whatever good conduct you find in me, that follow; whatever you do not find good, that do not follow." That is to say, the guru gives students freedom. He tells them to use their own judgment in deciding what is right and what is wrong. They are not to think that whatever their guru says is wholly right. It is certainly true that the guru is endeavoring to live by the truth, otherwise he would not be a guru; but he nevertheless cannot claim that his every action will be in harmony with truth. And so he tells his students to be alert, to use their intelligence and examine his conduct, and to disregard whatever seems to them wrong. And by this means he enables his students to grow into fearlessness.

Fearlessness means that we should neither fear anything, nor inflict fear on others. Both those things are parts of fearlessness. A tiger cannot be called fearless; it may not be afraid of any other animal, but it is afraid of a gun, and it also inspires fear in other creatures. True fearlessness neither enslaves another, nor does it slavishly submit to another.

The only sufficient basis for such fearlessness is the knowledge of the self. This self-knowledge is the foundation of education. But the education which children get today is the direct opposite of this. If a child commits some fault we slap it, and it begins to obey us because it is afraid. But we have taught it nothing of truth by our action. Until education is really based on fearlessness there is no hope of any change in society. We ought to teach children never to submit to those who bear and strike them.

No knowledge without action

The separation of learning from labor results also in social injustice. Some people do nothing but study and others nothing but hard labor, and as a result society is split in two. Those who earn their bread by manual labor form one social class and those who do only intellectual work form another. In India, manual laborers are paid one rupee a day, intellectual workers are paid twenty-five or thirty rupees. A very great injustice has been done by rating the value of manual and intellectual labor so differently. And it is the abolition of such injustice that must be the goal of our education.

Human lives are like trees, which cannot live if they are cut off from the soil, but at the same time the business of agriculture must be done so efficiently that the smallest possible number of people are tied entirely to the land. These two principles may seem to be mutually contradictory, but they are both parts of Basic Education. It is a basic need of humanity to be in touch with the earth, and any nation or civilization which is cut off from it slowly but surely loses its vigor and degenerates.

If a man's house is full of medicine bottles, we infer that the man is probably ill. But if his house is full of books, we conclude that he is intelligent. Surely that is not right? The first rule of health is to take medicine only when it is absolutely necessary. By the same token, the first rule of intelligence ought to be to avoid, so far as possible, burying one's eyes in books. We consider medicine bottles to be a sign of a sick body; we ought to consider books, whether secular or religious, as the sign of a sick mind!

Student-teacher comradeship

An interesting light is cast on the Indian attitude to education by the fact that in all fourteen languages of India there is no root word corresponding to English "teach." We can learn, we can help others to learn, but we cannot "teach." The use of two distinct words, "teach" and "learn," suggests that these two processes may be thought of as independent of one another. But that is merely the professional vanity of the "teacher," and we shall not understand the nature of education unless we rid ourselves of that vanity. Our first task is to realize that an "uneducated" human being is nowhere to be found. But today, all too often, an ordinary schoolboy treats a first-class carpenter as if he were an ignorant boor. The carpenter may be a man of maturity and experience, a wise and skilled workman, who is of real service to his community. But simply because he cannot read or write, the "educated" boy treats him as an inferior.

Wherever two people live together in this kind of comradeship, giving and receiving mutual help, there real education is in progress. The place of books is, therefore, secondary. This idea troubles many people, who think that if the place assigned to books is reduced the students will be deprived of the most valuable tools of knowledge. Books do have a place as tools of knowledge, but it is a very minor place. The major need is for teacher and student to become work-partners, and this can happen only when the distinction between the teacher "teaching" and the student "learning" can be overcome.

In matters of knowledge, no orders can be given. Education does not "discipline" students, it gives them complete freedom. Whether or not society free from governments is ever built in the larger world, such a society must be found in the world of students. If there is one thing of supreme importance for students, it is this freedom.

"Only teaching"

A young man said that he wished to do some good work for society.

"Tell me," I said, "what kind of work do you feel you could do well?"

"Only teaching, I think," replied the young man. "I can't do anything else, I can only teach, but I am interested in it and I feel sure that I shall be able to do it well."

"Yes, yes, I do not doubt that, but what are you going to teach? Spinning? Carding? Weaving? Could you teach any of these?"

"No, I can't teach those."

"Then tailoring, or dyeing, or carpentry?"

"No, I know nothing about them."

"Perhaps you could teach cooking, grinding, and other household skills?"

"No, I have never done any work like that. I can only teach..."

"My dear friend, you answer 'No' to every question, and yet you keep saying you can only teach. What do you mean? Can you teach gardening?"

The would-be teacher said, rather angrily, "Why do you ask all this? I told you at the beginning, I can do nothing else. I can teach literature."

"Good! Good! I am beginning to understand now. You mean you can teach people to write books like Tagore and Shakespeare?"

This made the young man so angry that he began to splutter.

"Take it easy," I laughed. "Can you teach patience?"

That was too much.

"I know what you mean," I said. "You can teach reading, writing, history, and geography. Well, they are not entirely useless, there are times in life when they are needed. But they are not basic to life. Would you be willing to learn weaving?"

"I don't want to learn anything new now. Besides I couldn't learn to weave, I have never before done any kind of handwork."

"In that case it might, of course, take you longer to learn, but why should you be unable to learn it?"

"I don't think I could ever learn it. But even supposing I could, it would mean a lot of hard work and a great deal of trouble. So please understand that I could not undertake it."

This conversation is quite enough to enable us to understand the psychology and characteristics of far too many of our "teachers." To be "only a teacher" means to be: completely ignorant of any kind of practical skill which might be useful in real life; incapable of learning anything new and indifferent towards any kind of craftsmanship; conceited; and buried in books. "Only teaching" means being a corpse cut off from life.

Government control of education is dangerous

Throughout the world education is under the control of governments. This is extremely dangerous. Governments ought to have no authority over education. The work of education should be in the hands of men of wisdom, but governments have got it in their grasp; every student in the country has to study whatever book is prescribed by the education department. If the government is fascist, students will be taught fascism; if it is communist, it will preach communism; if it is capitalist, it will proclaim the greatness of capitalism; if it believes in planning, the students will be taught all about planning. We in India used to hold to the principle that education should be completely free from state control. Kings exercised no authority over the gurus. The king had absolutely no power to control education. The consequence was that Sanskrit literature achieved a degree of freedom of thought such as can be seen nowhere else, so much so that no less than six mutually incompatible philosophies have arisen within the Hindu philosophy. This vigor is due to the freedom of education from state control.

The status of teachers has sunk so low that they feel themselves to have no authority at all. They must follow whatever path the government directs. They are under orders, the servants of authority. They may perhaps modify the government schemes by a comma here or a semi-colon there, but they cannot do more than that. Today there is an attempt to expand education, and the number of schools and of teachers is being increased, but the spirit of the true guru is not there. A good teacher means one who is a good servant; a bad teacher means a bad servant; good or bad, he remains a servant.

All this results from the fact that the education department is a government department, it is not independent. The judges of the high court are also appointed by the government, and they are bound by the laws which the government makes. Nevertheless, they are much more independent. They have power, within the bounds of law, to give a verdict against the government. The teacher ought to have a much greater freedom than the judge, yet today the education department is less independent than the department of justice.

The universities should demonstrate how every student, by his own labor, can gain food through knowledge and knowledge through food, nourishing his stomach with his two hands and his mind with his two eyes. They should show how the breach between knowledge and work can be closed. The students should have no fees to pay, there should be no hostel expenses and no salaries for the teachers. The workshop, the library and the laboratory should be provided by the government. There should be no need for holiday periods, for no one will feel any sense of confinement there.

The universities of today are not fitted for the poor, even though a few poor students may be admitted without fees as an act of grace. But the universities we envisage should be open to all. If the children of the rich cannot adjust themselves to such hard work, we may have to excuse them for an hour or two of labor as an act of grace.

Bought knowledge

If you ask someone what he is drinking he will answer "tea." There is sugar in it, but he never mentions the sugar, he never says he is drinking tea-and-sugar. The sweetness of the sugar permeates the tea, but the man drinks and says nothing about it. Education must be like the sugar, doing its work in secret. We can see the hands, nose, ears, eyes and tongue are active, but no one can see what the soul is doing. Our ears appear to be listening, our tongue appears to be talking. No matter what the appearance may be, it is not only the tongue that talks. In spite of appearances, it is not only the ears that hear. That which speaks and hears is the spirit within. And the spirit is invisible. The best education is similarly invisible. The more it is seen, the more imperfect it is.

4

Deschooling Society

Ivan Illich

Ivan Illich was born in 1926 in Vienna, Austria. After pursuing studies in the natural sciences, he obtained degrees in history, philosophy, and theology, and has lived and taught throughout the world. From 1962–76 he directed research seminars at the Center for Intercultural Documentation (CIDOC) in Cuernavaca where he still lives. His many books include Tools for Conviviality, Celebration of Awareness, Gender, Shadow Work, Limits to Medicine, Energy and Equity, ABC *and* Toward a History of Needs.

What follows is exerpted from the book of the same name that, when published in 1970, touched off a wave of interest in and debate about deschooling. Illich was an intellectual celebrity in the early seventies, and although he is rarely in the public view at present, he continues to write powerfully about a variety of subjects. Since this was written, Illich has revised his position on deschooling considerably, and he now takes a far more suspicious view of education as a contruct (see his foreword and the article by Aaron Falbel in this volume, as well as Ivan Illich in Conversation *with David Cayley, published by Anansi, 1992).* Deschooling Society *remains, however, one of the best books about schools ever written, and has been the entry point into deschooling for many people.*

Why we must disestablish school

MANY STUDENTS, ESPECIALLY THOSE WHO ARE POOR, INTUITIVELY know what the schools do for them. They school them to confuse process and substance. Once these become blurred, a new logic is assumed: the more treatment there is, the better are the results; or, escalation leads to success. The pupil is thereby "schooled" to confuse teaching with learning, grade advancement with education, a diploma with competence, and fluency with the ability to say something new. His imagination is "schooled" to accept service in place of value. Medical treatment is mistaken for health care, social work for the improvement of community life, police protection for safety, military poise for national security, the rat race for productive work. Health, learning, dignity, independence, and creative endeavor are defined as little more than the performance of the institutions which claim to serve these ends, and their improvement is made to depend on allocating more resources to the management of hospitals, schools, and other agencies in question.

I will show that the institutionalization of values leads inevitably to physical pollution, social polarization, and psychological impotence: three dimensions in a process of global degradation and modernized misery. I will explain how this process of degradation is accelerated when non-material needs are transformed into demands for commodities; when health, education, personal mobility, welfare, or psychological healing are defined as the result of services or "treatments." I do this because I believe that most of the research now going on about the future tends to advocate further increases in the institutionalization of values and that we must define conditions which would permit precisely the contrary to happen. We need research on the possible use of technology to create institutions which serve personal, creative, and autonomous interaction and emergence of values which cannot be substantially controlled by technocrats. We need counterfoil research to current futurology.

I want to raise the general question of the mutual definitions of man's nature and the nature of modern institutions which characterize our world view and language. To do so, I have chosen the school as my paradigm, and I therefore deal only indirectly with other bureaucratic agencies of the corporate state: the consumer-family, the party, the army, the church, the media. My analysis of the hidden curriculum of school should make it evident that public education would profit from the deschooling of society, just as family life, politics, security, faith, and communications would profit from an analogous process.

★

Not only education but social reality itself has become schooled. It costs roughly the same to school both rich and poor in the same dependency. The yearly expenditure per pupil in the slums and in the rich suburbs of any one of twenty U.S. cities lies in the same range—and sometimes is favorable to the poor. Rich and poor alike depend on schools and hospitals which guide their lives, form their world view, and define for them what is legitimate and what is not. Both view doctoring oneself as irresponsible, learning on one's own as unreliable, and community organization, when not paid for by those in authority, as a form of aggression or subversion. For both groups the reliance on institutional treatment renders independent accomplishment suspect. The progressive underdevelopment of self- and community-reliance is even more typical in Westchester than it is in the northeast of Brazil. Everywhere not only education but society as a whole needs "deschooling."

Equal educational opportunity is, indeed, both a desirable and a feasible goal, but to equate this with obligatory schooling is to confuse salvation with the Church. School has become the world religion of a modernized proletariat, and makes futile promises of salvation to the poor of the technological age. The nation-state has adopted it, drafting all citizens into a graded curriculum leading to sequential diplomas not unlike the initiation rituals and hieratic promotions of former times. The modern state has assumed the duty of enforcing the judgment of its educators through well-meant truant officers and job requirements, much as did the Spanish kings who enforced the judgments of their theologians through the conquistadors and the Inquisition.

Two centuries ago the United States led the world in a movement to disestablish the monopoly of a single church. Now we need the constitutional disestablishment of the monopoly of the school, and thereby of a system which legally combines prejudice and discrimination. . . .

★

Schools as false public utilities

Like highways, schools, at first glance, give the impression of being equally open to all comers. They are, in fact, open only to those who consistently renew their credentials. Just as highways create the impression that their present level of cost per year is necessary if people are to move, so schools are presumed essential for attaining the competence required by a society which uses modern technology. We have exposed speedways as spurious public utilities by noting their dependence on private automobiles. Schools are based upon the equally spurious hypothesis that learning is the result of curricular teaching.

Highways result from a perversion of the desire and need for mobility into the demand for a private car. Schools themselves pervert the natural inclination to grow and learn into the demand for instruction. Demand for manufactured maturity is a far greater abnegation of self-initiated activity than the demand for manufactured goods. Schools are not only to the right of highways and cars; they belong near the extreme of the institutional spectrum occupied by total asylums. Even the producers of body counts kill only bodies. By making men abdicate the responsibility for their own growth, school leads many to a kind of spiritual suicide.

Highways are paid for in part by those who use them, since tolls and gasoline taxes are extracted only from drivers. School, on the other hand, is a perfect system of regressive taxation, where the privileged graduates ride on the back of the entire paying public. School puts a head tax on promotion. The underconsumption of highway mileage is not nearly so costly as the underconsumption of schooling. The man who does not own a car in Los Angeles may be almost immobilized, but if he can somehow manage to reach a work place, he can get and hold a job. The school dropout has no alternative route. The suburbanite with his new Lincoln and his country cousin who drives a beat-up jalopy get essentially the same use out of the highway, even though one man's car costs thirty times more than the other's. The value of a man's schooling is a function of the number of years he has completed and of the costliness of the schools he has attended. The law compels no one to drive, whereas it obliges everyone to go to school.

5

Instead of Education

John Holt

John Holt (1923–1985) was a writer, educator, lecturer, and amateur musician who wrote ten books, including How Children Fail, How Children Learn, Never Too Late, Teach Your Own; *and* Freedom and Beyond. *His work has been translated into fourteen languages and* How Children Fail *has sold over a million copies in its many editions. The magazine he founded,* Growing Without Schooling, *and the associated organization, Holt Associates, keep his vision and legacy alive.*

Holt is the grandfather of the deschooling and homeschooling movements in North America. His remarkable personality and clear vision of an unschooled world is as poignant now as when it was written. Holt's work speaks to so many people in part because his thinking evolved very publicly through the course of ten books. The following pieces, excerpted from Instead of Education, *have been chosen from among literally dozens of brilliant books, essays, and lectures which Holt produced.*

THIS IS A BOOK IN FAVOR OF *DOING*—SELF-DIRECTED, PURPOSEFUL, meaningful life and work, and *against* "education"—learning cut off from active life and done under pressure of bribe or threat, greed and fear.

It is a book about people doing things, and doing them better; about the conditions under which we may be able to do things better; about some of the ways in which, *given those conditions*, other people may be able to help us (or we them) to do things better; and about the reasons why these conditions do not exist and *cannot be made to exist* within compulsory, coercive, competitive schools.

Not all persons will give the word "education" the meaning I give it here. Some may think of it, as I once described it, as "something a person gets for himself, not that which someone else gives or does to him." But I choose to define it here as most people do, something that some people do to others for their own good, molding and shaping them, and trying to make them learn what they think they ought to know. Today, everywhere in the world, that is what "education" has become, and I am wholly against it. People still spend a great deal of time—as for years I did myself— talking about how to make "education" more effective and efficient, or how to do it or give it to more people, or how to reform or humanize it. But to make it more effective and efficient will only be to make it worse, and to help it do even more harm. It cannot be reformed, cannot be carried out wisely or humanely, because its purpose is neither wise nor humane.

Next to the right to life itself, the most fundamental of all human rights is the right to control our own minds and thoughts. That means the right to decide for ourselves how we will explore the world around us, think about our own and other persons' experiences, and find and make the meaning of our own lives. Whoever takes that right away from us, as the educators do, attacks the very center of our being and does us a most profound and lasting injury. He tells us, in effect, that we cannot be trusted even to think, that for all our lives we must depend on others to tell us the meaning of our world and our lives, and that any meaning we may make for ourselves, out of our own experience, has no value.

Education, with its supporting system of compulsory and competitive schooling, all its carrots and sticks, its grades, diplomas, and credentials, now seems to me perhaps the most authoritarian and dangerous of all the social inventions of mankind. It is the deepest foundation of the modern and worldwide slave state, in which most people feel themselves to be nothing but producers, consumers, spectators, and "fans," driven more and more, in all parts of their lives, by greed, envy, and fear. My concern is not to improve "education" but to do away with it, to end the ugly and antihuman business of people-shaping and let people shape themselves.

By "doing" I do not mean only things done with the body, the muscles, with hands and tools, rather than with the mind alone. I am not trying to separate or put in opposition what many might call the "physical" and the "intellectual." Such distinctions are unreal and harmful. Only in words can the mind and body be separated. In reality they are one; they act together. So by "doing" I include such actions as talking, listening, writing, reading, thinking, even dreaming.

The point is that it is the do-er, not someone else, who has decided what he will say, hear, read, write, or think or dream about. He is at the center of his own actions. He plans, directs, controls, and judges them. He does them for his own purposes— which may, of course, include a common purpose with others. His actions are not ordered and controlled from outside. They belong to him and are a part of him.

This is not a book about such a doing society, or what it might be like. Enough to say that it would be a society whose tools and institutions would be much smaller in scale, serving human beings rather then being served by them; a society modest and sparing in its use of energy and materials, and reverent and loving in its attitude towards nature and the natural world. This is a book about how we might make the societies we have slightly more useful and livable for do-ers, about the resources that might help some people, at least, to lead more active and interesting lives— and, perhaps, to make some of the beginnings, or very small models, of such a society. It is not a book about how to solve or deal with such urgent problems as poverty, idleness, discrimination, exploitation, waste, and suffering. These are not education problems or school problems. They have not been and cannot and will not be solved by things done in compulsory schools, and they will not be solved by changing these schools (or even by doing away with them altogether). The most that may happen is that, once freed of the delusion that schools *can* solve these problems, we might begin to confront them directly, realistically, and intelligently.

The trouble with talk about "learning experiences" is that it implies that all experiences can be divided into two kinds, those from which we learn something, and those from which we learn nothing. But there are no experiences from which we learn nothing. We learn something from everything we do, and everything that happens to us or is done to us. What we learn may make us more informed or more ignorant, wiser or stupider, stronger or weaker, but we always learn something. What it is depends on the experience, and above all, on how we feel about it.

A central point of this book is that we are very unlikely to learn anything good from experiences which do not seem to us closely connected with what is interesting and important in the rest of our lives. Curiosity is never idle; it grows out of real concerns and real needs. Even more important, we are even less likely to learn anything good from coerced experiences, things that others have bribed, threatened, bullied, wheedled, or tricked us into doing. From such we learn mostly anger, resentment, and above all self-contempt and self-hatred for having allowed ourselves to be pushed around or used by others, for not having been smart enough or strong enough to resist and refuse. Some would claim that most people in their daily lives do a great many things—dull, repetitious, and meaningless work, driving a car for hours in traffic, watching television—from which they learn nothing. But of course they learn something. The people doing moronic work learn to hate that work, and themselves for having to do it—and, in time, all those who do not have to do it. The people driving cars in traffic learn to think of all the other people they see, driving or walking, as nuisances, obstructions, even as enemies, preventing them from getting where they want to go. And people watching television learn over and over again that the people they see on the screen, "real" or imaginary, are in every way better than they are—younger, handsomer, sexier, smarter, stronger, faster, braver, richer, happier, more successful and respected. When the time finally comes to come back from Dreamland to reality, and get up wearily and turn off the set, the thought is even more strongly in their minds, "Why couldn't I have been more like them?"

Doing is learning

Another common and mistaken idea hidden in the word "learning" is that learning and doing are different kinds of acts. Thus, not many years ago I began to play the cello. I love the instrument, spend many hours a day playing it, work hard at it, and mean someday to play it well. Most people would say that what I am doing is "learning to play the cello." Our language gives us no other words to say it. But these words carry into our minds the strange idea that there exists two different processes: (1) learning to play the cello; and (2) playing the cello. They imply that I will do the first until I have completed it, at which point I will stop the first process and begin the second; in short, that I will go on "learning to play" until I "have learned to play," and that then I will begin "to play."

Of course, this is nonsense. There are not two processes, but one. We learn to do something by doing it. There is no other way. When we first do something, we probably will not do it well. But if we keep on doing it, have good models to follow and helpful advice if and when we feel we need it, and always do it as well as we can, we will do it better. In time, we may do it very well. This process never ends. The finest musicians, dancers, athletes, surgeons, pilots, or whatever they may be, must constantly practise their art or craft. Every day the musicians do their scales, the dancers exercise at the barre, and so on. A surgeon I knew would from time to time, when not otherwise busy, tie knots in fine surgical gut with one hand, without looking, just to keep in practice. In that sense, people never stop "learning to do" what they know how to do, no matter how well they do it. They must "learn" every day to do it as well as they can, or they will soon do it less well. The principal flutist of the Boston Symphony under Koussevitsky used to say, "If I miss a day's practice, I hear the difference; if I miss two days', the conductor hears the difference; if I miss three days', the audience hears the difference."

Sam Roddick

Part Two — Living Fully: More Recent Analysis

6

Sweet Land of Liberty

Grace Llewellyn

Grace Llewellyn is a former middle school English teacher who taught in Oakland and Berkeley in California, in Boise, Idaho, and in Colorado. She has since left schools and become a full-time unschooling advocate, writing and publishing The Teenage Liberation Handbook *and* Real Lives. *She also publishes a newsletter,* Unschooling Ourselves, *and is presently at work on a new book about leaving school and getting a great job. She lives in Eugene, Oregon.*

In recent years Grace has become one of our most important deschooling advocates. Her two books are immensely popular among homelearners and her voice is one that is consistently approachable, direct, and clear. She has done much to bring unschooling to teenagers, and The Teenage Liberation Handbook *(1991), from which these excerpts are drawn, remains the best guide I know of for step-by-step deschooling. Either of her books makes a great present for any teenager.*

THE MOST OVERWHELMING REALITY OF SCHOOL IS CONTROL. School controls the way you spend your time (what is life made of if not time?), how you behave, what you read, and to a large extent what you think. In school you can't control your own life. Outside of school you can, at least to the extent that your parents trust you to. "Comparing me to those who are conventionally schooled," writes twelve-year-old unschooler Colin Roch, "is like comparing the freedoms of a wild stallion to those of cattle in a feedlot."

The ultimate goal of this book is for you to start associating the concept of freedom with you, and to start wondering why you and your friends don't have much of it, and for you to move out of the busy-prison into the meadows of life. There are lots of good reasons to quit school, but in my idealistic American mind, the pursuit of freedom encompasses most of them and outshines the others.

If you look at the history of "freedom," you notice that the most frightening thing about people who are not free is that they learn to take their bondage for granted, and to believe that this bondage is "normal" and natural.

Right now, a lot of you are helping history to repeat itself; you don't believe you should be free. Of course you want to be free—in various ways, not just free of school. However, society gives you so many condescending, false, and harmful messages about yourselves that most of you wouldn't trust yourselves with freedom. It's all complicated by the fact that the people who infringe most dangerously and inescapably on your freedom are those who say they are helping you, those who are convinced you need their help: teachers, school counselors, perhaps your parents.

Why should you have freedom?

Why should anyone? To become human, to live fully. Insofar as you live what someone else dictates, you do not live. Choice is a fundamental essence of life, and in the fullest life, each choice is deliberate and savored.

Another reason you should be free is obvious. You should learn to live responsibly and joyfully in a free country.

Recently, school people talk a lot about "experiential education." Educators have wisely realized that the best way to teach anything includes not only reading about a subject, but also practising it. For example, my colleague Gary Oakley taught science by having students rehabilitate a polluted pond. Naturally, learning this way sinks in deeper than merely reading, hearing lectures, and discussing. It means participating—being a scientist or musician rather than watching from the outside.

What the educators apparently haven't realized yet is that experiential education is a double-edged sword. If you do something to learn it, then what you do, you learn. All the time you are in school, you learn through experience how to live in a dictatorship. In school you shut your notebook when the bell rings. You do not speak unless granted permission. You are guilty until proven innocent, and who will prove you innocent? You are told what to do, think, and say for six hours a day. If your teacher says sit up and pay attention, you had better stiffen your spine and try to get Bobby or Sally or the idea of Spring or the play you're writing off your mind. The most constant and thorough thing students in school experience—and learn—is the antithesis of democracy.

Authority

Regardless of what the law or your teacher have to say about this, you are as human as anyone over the age of eighteen or twenty-one. Yet "minors" are one of the most oppressed groups of people in the United States, and certainly the most discriminated against legally.

It starts at home. Essentially, your parent can require you to do almost anything and forbid you to do almost anything. Fortunately, most parents try hard not to abuse this power. Yet, from a legal standpoint, the reason schools have so much tyrannical power over you is that they act *in loco parentis*—in place of the parent. As legal parental substitutes, they can search your locker or purse, tell you to be quiet, read your mail (notes), sometimes hit or "spank" you, speak rudely to you, and commit other atrocities—things I hope your parent(s) would not do with a clean conscience, and things no sensible adult would do to another adult, for fear of losing a job or ending a friendship.

Many teenagers, of course, do clash with their parents to some extent. But most parents like and love their children enough to listen to their side, grant them most freedoms as they grow, back off when they realize they're overbearing, and generally behave reasonably. The schools may do this with some "rebellious" students, but not usually, and not after a second or third "offence." Schools are too big, and the adults in them too overworked, to see "rebels" as people—instead, they'll get a permanent-ink "bad person" label and unreasonable treatment. Even in a small private school, authority is often unyielding and unfairly judgmental.

When I was substitute teaching in Oakland, California, I was told I could have a month-long job teaching choir and piano while the regular teacher had a baby. As it happened, I did have a fairly substantial musical background and could have handled at least that aspect of the job just fine. But the administrators showed no interest in my musical knowledge—all they wanted was someone who could maintain order for a month. When the principal introduced me to the choir class, one of the students raised his hand and asked, "Since she's not a music teacher, what are we supposed to do if she's not any good?"

The principal launched into a tirade about how it doesn't matter what you think of her teaching, you'll do exactly what she says and I don't want to hear about any problems from any of you; the state board of education decided she was good enough to be certified and that's all you need to know.

One of the worst things about this sort of arbitrary authority is it makes us lose our trust of natural authority—people who know what they're doing and could share a lot of wisdom with us. When they make you obey the cruel and unreasonable teacher, they steal your desire to learn from the kind and reasonable teacher. When they tell you to be sure to pick up after yourselves in the cafeteria, they steal your own natural sense of courtesy.

Many times, I have heard teachers resort defiantly to the proclamation: "The bottom line is, they need to do what we tell them because they're the kids and we're the adults." This concept that teenagers should obey simply because of their age no longer makes any sense to me. I can't figure out what it is based on, except adults' own egos. In this regard, school often seems like a circus arena full of authority-craving adults. Like trained animals, you are there to make them look good, to help them believe they are better than you.

Because they can never make you free, schools can never allow you to learn fully.

Love of learning

If you had always been free to learn, you would follow your natural tendency to find out as fully as possible about the things that interest you, cars or stars. We are all born with what they call "love of learning," but it dives off into an elusive void when we go to school.

Of course, quitting school doesn't guarantee that you are going to learn more in every subject than you did in school. If you hate math in school, and decide to continue studying it outside of school, it's possible that you won't enjoy it any more or learn it much better, although being able to work without ridicule at your own speed will help. You will see a dramatically wonderful change in the way you learn about the things that interest you. What's more, you will find out that you are interested in things that haven't yet caught your attention, and that you can love at least some of the things which repulsed you in school.

Beyond the love and pursuit of something specific, there's another quality you might also call love of learning. It's simple curiosity, which kills more tired assumptions than kills cats. Some people move around with their ears and eyes perked open like raccoons, ready to find out something new and like it. Do everything you can to cultivate this characteristic; it will enliven your life immeasurably.

7

The Public School Nightmare: Why Fix a System Designed to Destroy Individual Thought?

John Taylor Gatto

John Taylor Gatto was a Manhattan school teacher for almost thirty years. He was named New York City's Teacher of the Year in 1990, and State Teacher of the Year in 1991. He has spoken at the White House, at Yale, at scores of institutions, on dozens of television and radio shows, and to packed halls across the continent. He has taught at Cornell and California State, is a heavy pistol champion, a garlic farmer, a national authority on adoption, a chess player, and a talker of some repute. His two books, Dumbing Us Down *and* The Exhausted School, *are both widely available.*

John is one of the most compelling writers about schools today. His thinking is informed by more than two decades as a New York City public school teacher, and his perspective is deeply entrenched in American ideals of liberty and freedom. His commentary, specifically when talking about turning schools over to the free market, is considered by some to be right-wing. It is salutary, however, to consider the libertarian, radically democratic tradition from which his thinking has evolved. He is a genuinely inspiring person, and his vision is remarkably clear. The following is taken from a talk delivered to the Conference on Private Initiatives in Education, held in Indianapolis in 1991.

I WANT YOU TO CONSIDER THE FRIGHTENING POSSIBILITY THAT WE ARE spending far too much money on schooling, not too little. I want you to consider that we have too many people employed in interfering with the way children grow up—and that all this money and all these people, all the time we take out of children's lives and away from their homes and families and neighborhoods and private explorations gets in the way of education.

That seems radical, I know. Surely in modern technological society it is the quantity of schooling and the amount of money you spend on it that buys value. And yet last year in St. Louis, I heard a vice-president of IBM tell an audience of people assembled to redesign the process of teacher certification that in his opinion this country became computer-literate by self-teaching, not through any action of schools. He said 45 million people were comfortable with computers who had learned through dozens of non-systematic strategies, none of them very formal; if schools had pre-empted the right to teach computer use we would be in a horrible mess right now instead of leading the world in this literacy.

Now think about Sweden, a beautiful, healthy, prosperous and up-to-date country with a spectacular reputation for quality in everything it produces. It makes sense to think their schools must have something to do with that. Then what do you make of the fact that you can't go to school in Sweden until you are seven years old? The reason the unsentimental Swedes have wiped out what would be first and seconds grades here is that they don't want to pay the large social bill that quickly comes due when boys and girls are ripped away from their best teachers at home too early.

It just isn't worth the price, say the Swedes, to provide jobs for teachers and therapists if the result is sick, incomplete kids who can't be put back together again very easily. The entire Swedish school sequence isn't twelve years, either—it's nine. Less schooling, not more. The direct savings of such a step in the United States would be $75–100 billion—a lot of unforeclosed home mortgages, a lot of time freed up with which to seek an education.

Who was it that decided to force your attention onto Japan instead of Sweden? Japan with its long school year and state compulsion, instead of Sweden with its short school year, short school sequence, and free choice where your kid is schooled? Who decided you should know about Japan and not Hong Kong, an Asian neighbor with a short school year that outperforms Japan across the board in math and science? Whose interests are served by hiding that from you?

One of the principal reasons we got into the mess we're in is that we allowed schooling to become a very profitable monopoly, guaranteed its customers by the police power of the state. Systematic schooling attracts increased investment only when it does poorly, and since there are no penalties at all for such performance, the temptation not to do well is overwhelming. That's because school staffs, both line and management, are involved in a guild system; in that ancient form of association no single member is allowed to outperform any other member, is allowed to advertise or is allowed to introduce new technology or improvise without the advance consent of the guild. Violation of these precepts is severely sanctioned—as Marva Collins, Jaime Escalante and a large number of once-brilliant teachers found out.

The guild reality cannot be broken without returning primary decision-making to parents, letting them buy what they want to buy in schooling, and encouraging the entrepreneurial reality that existed until 1852. That is why I urge any business to think twice before entering a cooperative relationship with the schools we currently have. Cooperating with these places will only make them worse.

The structure of American schooling, 20th century style, began in 1806 when Napoleon's amateur soldiers beat the professional soldiers of Prussia at the battle of Jena. When your business is selling soldiers, losing a battle like that is serious. Almost immediately afterwards, a German philosopher named Fichte delivered his famous "Address to the German Nation" which became one of the most influential documents in modern history. In effect he told the Prussian people that the party was over, that the nation would have to shape up through a new utopian institution of forced schooling in which everyone would learn to take orders.

So the world got compulsion schooling at the end of a state bayonet for the first time in human history; modern forced schooling started in Prussia in 1819 with a clear vision of what centralized schools could deliver:
  1) obedient soldiers to the army;
  2) obedient workers to the mines;
  3) well subordinated civil servants to government;

4) well subordinated clerks to industry;

5) citizens who thought alike about major issues.

Schools, according to Fichte, should create an artificial national consensus on matters that had been worked out in advance by leading German families and the head of institutions. Schools should create unity among all the German states, eventually unifying them into Greater Prussia.

Prussian industry boomed from the beginning. Prussia was successful in warfare and her reputation in international affairs was very high. Twenty-six years after this form of schooling began, the King of Prussia was invited to North America to determine the boundary between the United States and Canada. Thirty-three years after that fateful invention of the central school institution, at the behest of Horace Mann and many other leading citizens, we borrowed the style of Prussian schooling as our own.

You need to know this because, over the first 50 years of our school institution, Prussian purpose—which was to create a form of state socialism—gradually forced out traditional American purpose, which in most minds was to prepare the individual to be self-reliant.

In Prussia the purpose of the *Volksschule*, which educated 92 percent of the children, was not intellectual development at all, but socialization in obedience and subordination. Thinking was left to the *Real Schulen*, in which eight percent of the kids participated. But for the great mass, intellectual development was regarded with managerial horror, as something that caused armies to lose battles.

Prussia concocted a method based on complex fragmentations to ensure that its school products would fit the grand social design. Some of this method involved dividing whole ideas into school subjects, each further divisible, some of it involved short periods punctuated by a horn so that self-motivation in study would be muted by ceaseless interruptions.

There were many more techniques of training, but all were built around the premise that isolation from first-hand information, and fragmentation of the abstract information presented by teachers, would result in obedient and subordinate graduates, properly respectful of arbitrary orders. "Lesser" men would be unable to interfere with policy makers because, while they could still complain, they could not manage sustained or comprehensive thought. Well-schooled children cannot think critically, cannot argue effectively.

One of the most interesting by-products of Prussian schooling turned out to be the two most devastating wars of modern history. Erich Maria Remarque, in his classic *All Quiet on the Western Front*, tells us that the First World War was caused by the tricks of schoolmasters, and the famous Protestant theologian Dietrich Bonhoeffer said that the Second World War was the inevitable product of good schooling.

It's important to underline that Bonhoeffer meant that literally, not metaphorically: schooling after the Prussian fashion removes the ability of the mind to think for itself. It teaches people to wait for a teacher to tell them what to do and if what they have done is good or bad. Prussian teaching paralyses the moral will as well as the intellect. It's true that sometimes well-schooled students sound smart, because they memorize many opinions of great thinkers, but they actually are badly damaged because their own ability to think is left rudimentary and undeveloped.

We got from the United States to Prussia and back because a small number of very passionate ideological leaders visited Prussia in the first half of the 19th century, and fell in love with the order, obedience, and efficiency of its system and relentlessly proselytized for a translation of Prussian vision onto these shores. If Prussia's ultimate goal was the unification of Germany, our major goal, so these men thought, was the unification of hordes of immigrant Catholics into a national consensus based on a northern European cultural model. To do that, children would have to be removed from their parents and from inappropriate cultural influences.

In this fashion, compulsion schooling, a bad idea that had been around at least since Plato's *Republic*, a bad idea that New England had tried to enforce in 1650 without any success, was finally rammed through the Massachusetts legislature in 1852. It was, of course, the famous "Know-Nothing" legislature that passed this law, a legislature that was the leading edge of a famous secret society which flourished at that time known as The Order of the Star Spangled Banner, whose password was the simple sentence, "I know nothing"—hence the popular label attached to the secret society's political arm, The American Party.

Over the next 50 years, state after state followed suit, ending schools of choice and ceding the field to a new government monopoly. There was one powerful exception to this—the children who could afford to be privately educated.

It's important to note that the underlying premise of Prussian schooling is that the government is the true parent of children—the state is sovereign over the family. At the most extreme pole of this notion is the idea that biological parents are really the enemies of their own children, not to be trusted.

How did a Prussian system of dumbing children down take hold in American schools? Thousands and thousands of young men from prominent American families journeyed to Prussia and other parts of Germany during the 19th century and brought home the PhD degree to a nation in which such a credential was unknown. These men pre-empted the top positions in the academic world, in corporate research, and in government, to the point where opportunity was almost closed to those who had not studied in Germany, or who were not the direct disciples of a German PhD, as John Dewey was the disciple of G. Stanley Hall at Johns Hopkins.

Virtually every single one of the founders of American schooling had made the pilgrimage to Germany, and many of these men wrote widely circulated reports praising the Teutonic methods. Horace Mann's famous "Seventh Report" of 1844, still available in large libraries, was perhaps the most important of these.

By 1889, a little more than 100 years ago, the crop was ready for harvest. In that year the U.S. Commissioner of Education, William Torrey Harris, assured a railroad magnate, Collis Huntington, that American schools were "scientifically designed" to prevent "over-education" from happening. The average American would be content with his humble role in life, said the commissioner, because he would not be tempted to think about any other role. My guess is that Harris meant he would not be able to think about any other role.

In 1896 the famous John Dewey, then at the University of Chicago, said that independent, self-reliant people were a counter-productive anachronism in the collective society of the future. In modern society, said Dewey, people would be defined by their associations—not by their own individual accomplishments. In such a world people who read too well or too early are dangerous because they become privately empowered, they know too much, and know how to find out what they don't know by themselves, without consulting experts.

Dewey said the great mistake of traditional pedagogy was to make reading and writing constitute the bulk of early schoolwork. He advocated that the phonics method of teaching reading be abandoned and replaced by the whole word method, not because the latter was more efficient (he admitted that it was less efficient) but because independent thinkers were produced by hard books, thinkers who cannot be socialized very easily. By socialization, Dewey meant a program of social objectives administered by the best social thinkers in government. This was a giant step on the road to state socialism, the form pioneered in Prussia, and it is a vision radically disconnected with the American past, its historic hopes and dreams.

Dewey's former professor and close friend, G. Stanley Hall, said this at about the same time, "Reading should no longer be a fetish. Little attention should be paid to reading." Hall was one of the three men most responsible for building a gigantic administrative infrastructure over the classroom. How enormous that structure really became can only be understood by comparisons: New York State, for instance, employs more school administrators than all of the European Economic Community nations combined.

Once you think that the control of conduct is what schools are about, the word "reform" takes on a very particular meaning. It means making adjustments to the machine so that young subjects will not twist and turn so, while their minds and bodies are being scientifically controlled. Helping kids to use their minds better is beside the point.

Bertrand Russell once observed that American schooling was among the most radical experiments in human history, that America was deliberately denying its children the tools of critical thinking. When you want to teach children to think, you begin by treating them seriously when they are little, giving them responsibilities, talking to them candidly, providing privacy and solitude for them, and making them readers and thinkers of significant thoughts from the beginning. That's if you want to teach them to think. There is no evidence that this has been a state purpose since the start of compulsion schooling.

When Friedrich Froebel, the inventor of kindergarten in 19th century Germany, fashioned his idea, he did not have a "garden for children" in mind, but a metaphor of teachers as gardeners and children as the vegetables. Kindergarten was created to be a way to break the influence of mothers on their children. I note with interest the growth of daycare in the United States and the repeated urgings to extend school downward to include four-year-olds. The movement toward state socialism is not some historical curiosity but a powerful dynamic force in the world around us. It is fighting for its life against those forces which would, through vouchers or tax credits, deprive it of financial lifeblood, and it has countered this thrust with a demand for even more control over children's lives, and even more money to pay for the extended school day and year that this control requires.

A movement as visibly destructive to individuality, family and community as government-system schooling has been might be expected to collapse in the face of its dismal record, coupled with an increasingly aggressive shakedown of the taxpayer, but this has not happened. The explanation is largely found in the transformation of schooling from a simple service to families and towns to an enormous, centralized corporate enterprise.

While this development has had a markedly adverse effect on people and on our democratic traditions, it has made schooling the single largest employer in the United States, and the largest granter of contracts next to the Defence Department. Both of these low-visibility phenomena provide monopoly schooling with powerful political friends, publicists, advocates, and other useful allies. This is a large part of the explanation why no amount of failure ever changes things in schools, or changes them for very long. School people are in a position to outlast any storm and to keep short-attention-span public scrutiny thoroughly confused.

An overview of the short history of this institution reveals a pattern marked by intervals of public outrage, followed by enlargement of the monopoly in every case.

★

After nearly 30 years spent inside a number of public schools, some considered good, some bad, I feel certain that management cannot clean its own house. It relentlessly marginalizes all significant change. There are no incentives for the "owners" of the structure to reform it, nor can there be without outside competition.

It cannot be overemphasized that no body of theory exists to define accurately the way children learn, or which learning is of most worth. By pretending the existence of such, we have cut ourselves off from the information and innovation that only a real market can provide. Fortunately our national situation has been so favorable, so dominant through most of our history, that the margin of error afforded has been vast.

But the future is not so clear. Violence, narcotic addictions, divorce, alcoholism, loneliness—all these are but tangible measures of a poverty in education. Surely schools, as the institutions monopolizing the daytimes of childhood, can be called to account for this. In a democracy the final judges cannot be experts, but only the people.

Trust the people, give them choices, and the school nightmare will vanish in a generation.

8

Challenging the Popular Wisdom: What Can Families Do?

Geraldine Lyn-Piluso, Gus Lyn-Piluso, and Duncan Clarke

Geraldine and Gus Lyn-Piluso live in Toronto where they facilitate a number of community-based workshops on parenting, education, child-development, and sports. Geraldine, who plays on a competitive touch football team, is an Associate Faculty Member in the Education Department at Goddard College in Vermont. She is working also on her doctorate in education and teaches part-time at an independent alternative school. Gus received his PhD in Education from the Union Institute, is an Early Childhood Education professor at Seneca College in Toronto and coaches soccer and touch football teams. They have two daughters, Caileigh and Joey.

Duncan Clarke is currently living and working in Marietta, Pennsylvania. With an MA in Education from Goddard College, he has recently been writing about education, critical pedagogy, anarchism, and deschooling. Duncan is also helping to homeschool his elementary-aged nieces, and makes wicked pretzels.

This article, created with Duncan specifically for this anthology, is part of an ongoing project Geraldine and Gus have undertaken to define an egalitarian, deschooled, childrearing ethic. Their style and approach make an important complement to many of the others in this anthology, and are critical in defining the radical potential of families and children.

FAMILY. WHAT DO WE TALK ABOUT WHEN WE TALK ABOUT FAMILY? Our lives—our past or present circumstances, our loves, our hurts, our life choices, and philosophies. A mélange of stories and people and relations, richly diverse, sometimes tender, often not. The nervous (and increasingly nasty) struggle by cultural conservatives to force their own narrow definition of the family on this shifting assortment of living arrangements signifies a bundle of hot-button anxieties: about gender and sexual orientation, abortion, sex, race and class, male privilege. Not coincidentally, these same issues have served to catalyze major modern movements of liberation; consequently, "family values" has become a coded phrase for the home front in the ongoing culture wars.

And "family values" means, of course, kids—precious, obedient, little spittin' images. But the Right's attempt to dictate their retrograde ideology betrays a suspicion that no amount of sentimental rhetoric can hide: a fear that children—the heart of the nuclear family—are potentially radical. This suspicion is well-founded. Kids, as anyone who takes them seriously can attest, often demonstrate an ability to draw attention to the underlying political dimension of everyday life—to the dubious pretences by which authority, including parental authority, establishes itself.

Without censure, with the room to be confidently inquisitive and direct, kids may discern the fundamentals of social relations by unearthing the root, or radical, details which betray the reality of those relations—reminding us, time and again, of the hidden strangling roots of power from which our society draws its authority. Spying that loose edge, they may just pry it back to ask: Why? Why do my sneakers say 'Made in Pakistan'? Why are the sidewalks in this part of town crumbling? Why are we supposed to go to school?

Authoritarian or egalitarian?

What does this ability mean? It means that children haven't quite consented to a society organized on the basis of oppression, for one thing. It also presents parents and other caregivers with a definite choice. On the one hand, we can induce children to blunt their concerns, to concede to domination as an inevitable and immutable state of affairs in the home or the classroom, and so secure our own rule (and ultimately, hierarchy itself). In short, we can crush the radical potential of childhood the moment it arises. On the other hand, we may nurture this ability which, as it matures, makes it possible to imagine a better world. Nurture it how? By allowing and encouraging children to challenge any authority which would compel them to surrender their consent.

This means that we commit ourselves to nothing short of a dialogue, since by agitating our certainties with perfectly sensible questions, kids prod us to examine our own authority. They also remind us that, in the face of unjustifiable authority, we adults too often and too easily acquiesce. The result? A cooperative exploration of power, society, and the natural world—an adventure which constitutes deschooling.

Here we ought to distinguish deschooling from homeschooling. Deschooling begins with the radical appraisal of compulsory schooling. In common with other educational reform movements, the inability of the present school system to actually "educate" is exposed. However, deschoolers reject the present schooling system because of its inherently authoritarian nature; and this staunchly anti-authoritarian critique is where deschooling parts ways with the 'homeschooling' movement. Many homeschooling families reject the school system, yet maintain authoritarian family structures and in fact implement authoritarian pedagogical techniques within the home. While such families admittedly challenge the school system, the intent of the challenge is to demand that schools adhere more rigidly to their authoritarian ways, in order to annihilate the child's subversive inclinations.

This reactionary position may offer short term advantages, but in the long run it serves to strengthen our hierarchical society. Deschooling does not simply move the school to home—it rejects the school and its authoritarian nature completely. It aims at the full development of human beings who "own" themselves, who are critically conscious, free individuals committed to social transformation.

Deschooling, then, means more than just protecting kids from the coercive policies of the school. It's a way of parenting, a critique of the family, and a genuinely mutual endeavor—requiring a dialogue among parents (or other caregivers) and children, as well as a conscious effort to de-professionalize learning by acknowledging it as a lifelong, cooperative project of questioning and discovery, thinking and rethinking. In stark contrast to the traditional authoritarian family structure, deschooling demands egalitarian relations between parents and kids—a family organization which accommodates the radical curiosity of childhood, even (perhaps especially) when it challenges authority. Parenting, in the deschooling family, becomes a revolutionary activity.

The challenges of deschooling

The hurdles deschoolers face are formidable. For instance, working vigorously to discourage kids from questioning anything deeply are institutions of explicit power, such as school and government and capitalist business, which rationalize their exploits with a credo so effective it eventually becomes simple, incontrovertible, common sense. What's common sense? That set of implicit assumptions which is not to be doubted—that bedrock of unyielding and unexamined convictions we may run up against when, for instance, we attempt to explain deschooling to a resistant friend or colleague or grandparent.

"But you've got to think about socialization," we hear, "you've got to think about academics!" —as if the basic childhood activities of learning and socializing depended on state-mandated institutions. Absurd? Of course. Among adults, this impasse—encountered when we question what is generally acknowledged as unquestionable—bears testimony to the power that dominant institutions employ in shaping our view of the world.

Until they're "properly" trained, however, kids don't know what not to question; as a result, their artless queries can cut deep, exposing authority's most damning contradictions. As we've pointed out, this indicates a radical potential in childhood. At the very least, such questions deserve our honest response. Scorned, or deterred, the inquisitive child learns to regard the world as incomprehensible, not worth questioning—and thus unchangeable.

Here the challenges of deschooling become intricate, because, before receiving an answer, children deserve something even more basic: the opportunity to ask the question. We would be naive to consider this a simple, naturally-occurring thing. It takes a good deal of savvy, as well as a sense of humor, to give a child's searing, point-blank curiosity its due; and as we know, occasions for genuine inquiry are routinely obstructed by professionalized education and the corporately-dispensed culture of the various mainstream media, with the goal of confining the child's potentially subversive curiosity to suit their own purposes.

In other words, the opportunity to ask the radical question is the very opportunity these institutions struggle to interrupt; and it is the opportunity that we—as caring adults—ought to provide and nurture, so that curiosity may flourish. Because it forces us to side either with or against institutions of power, the way we care for children is, among other things, a political act.

It's also a responsibility which demands a detailed awareness of the political landscape. To cite an example: in the United States, Federal Communication Commission (FCC) rulings of 1983 and 1984 lifted all children's programming guidelines, including those restricting the length and number of TV commercials aimed at kids. As a direct result, during the last ten years increasingly sophisticated marketing efforts targeting pre-teens have painstakingly constructed a universe of products whose every loose corner has been seemingly nailed tight: films tied in to television series tied in to action figures tied in to cereal box loot tied in to video game cartridges tied in to school lunch packs tied in to fast food prizes tied in to blanket sleepers tied in to disposable dinnerware, and on and on. The goal, obviously, is to diminish the child's opportunity to pose any questions which may spoil the plastic pretense—to obliterate all traces of those strangling roots of power. Take a look around, kid. It's a Disney world—you just live in it. So join the fun, shut up, and buy.

A space for creative inquiry

Caught in the shadow of such institutional monoliths, how can we live according to our principles, especially beyond the confines of our home? Let's admit that retreating to a safe haven—through isolation, avoidance of mass culture, unplugging the TV—hardly solves the problem. Not only is it a quixotic goal, a kind of self-delusion, it also fails to answer the simple question of what we do when, for instance, a niece requests a Sun Beach Barbie for her birthday.

Maybe we give in—buy it, make her happy, and win temporary status as a favorite uncle or aunt. Or we flat out refuse, take a deep breath, and—at the risk of sounding tedious—explain that the purchase of one Barbie doll reinforces our sexist society, perpetuates consumerism, exploits the labor of underpaid wage workers, and secures yet another piece of plastic for an overflowing landfill.

Or, less pedantically, we draw out the radical potential in this fragile moment, not with a lecture or an interrogation, but with candid, open-ended talk. That is, we gently rouse the spirit of critical inquiry which Mattel, with its vision of pink, polished, ecstatic blondness, has struggled to obliterate from our niece's psyche.

Why Sun Beach Barbie? Uh-huh. And where did you hear about her? What do you think of the actors in the Barbie commercial? Yeah, me, too. How much do you think Barbie costs? How many hours do you think an employee in a Barbie factory would have to work in order to afford a Barbie doll? No, I don't quite know either. Does it matter? And what kind of lifestyle would Sun Beach Barbie lead? How would she pay for it? Would it be fun? What's "fun" mean?

The issues are the fundamental sort that children regularly contemplate. Trying to make sense out of a paradoxical world, kids are neither completely free nor wholly dominated; after a few playful exchanges, even the most TV-addled kid may begin disputing corporate authority with considerable enthusiasm. Our responsibility lies in providing a space for creative inquiry. And, of course, for dialogue—for in the end, we might find ourselves facing a few equally pointed questions. ("Uh yeah, I used to have a Barbie. Yea, I guess she was kind of fun...") Admittedly, a life of sand, surf, and endless leisure has some appeal. We may even be forced to rethink our political convictions, as well as our parental authority, since a child's eye for the hidden political dimension is guileless—it can unmask all sorts of pretense, including principled affectation.

Family, politics and authority

The political dimension of childrearing comes to the fore in such encounters, which are obviously risky. They are also rarely discussed. For example, while general-interest bookstores are well-stocked with an abundance of childrearing and educational manuals, the standard glossy trade paperback offers very little on the political nature of parenting. Rather, we're instructed how to toilet train our children in a day, help them read in thirty, hone their competitive edge by enrolling them in this week's computer whiz-kid class, and so forth. All this depends, of course, on our becoming proficient in the latest behavior management techniques. Deeper questions—concerning our existence, our society and its relation to the natural world, and the nature of our institutions—remain largely unacknowledged.

This oversight shows a misunderstanding of children, who are captivated by the deeper questions. But the subject of authority—that is, the institution of society—is regularly neglected, even by genuinely caring parents; and this is at least understandable. For when children are encouraged to ponder the legitimacy of power and authority, the authority of family structure inevitably comes under scrutiny. And there, for many adults, the conversation ends with, "Because I said so."

This phrase is famously effective; it appeals, after all, to the parents' indisputable might. Here we once again confront the political responsibilities of the deschooling parent, and the reality of an oppressive political institution much closer to home: the family. As numerous radical social thinkers have argued, the conflation of authority with might—the very basis of the patriarchal family—is crucial to the development of the obedient, fearful, authoritarian personality, and the authoritarian personality, in turn, forms the backbone of a society organized according to the hierarchical tenet of dominance and submission.

If the adult caregivers appeal to patriarchal rule and physical force, if they encourage docility and demand unquestioning homage to their own authority, if they express parental love through destructive self-sacrifice, their demands neatly dovetail with the demands of the state and the workplace. In short, the family—even more so than the school—serves the needs of an oppressive social, political, and economic order; historically, it has done so with appalling success, generating millions of pliant citizens quite willing to sacrifice their lives to defend and maintain the instruments of their own oppression.

But as we've seen, the social impact of family structure works both ways. That is, if the traditional family is a powerful force, then a more communal and egalitarian childrearing arrangement can act as a powerfully subversive force, challenging those institutions organized along lines of command and obedience—institutions which propagate the self-serving notion that egalitarian social organization is impractical, if not preposterous. This bleak ideology sediments into a general, widespread belief that any society ensuring collective decision-making is impossible. But what "impossible" really means in this context is: inconceivable to the conventional thinker. The work of people striving to revolutionize family structure allows the suggestion of such a society to take shape in the imagination.

Toward a deschooled society

Let's develop our description of this potential society, and its prefiguration in alternative means of childrearing, by explaining a few principles of deschooling.

A unified conception of childrearing, education, and human development: The word "educate" derives from the Latin *educare*, meaning "to nourish, to cause to grow;" originally it retained this organic connotation in English. Deschooling reclaims the origins of the word. Education, then, does not start at the arbitrary age of six, nor does it end with high school or college; education is the act of living and growing, of consciously responding to and manipulating one's environment based on experience and reflection. This definition recalls John Dewey's notion of learning by doing, except that in deschooling, the child—not the teacher—ultimately directs the process.

Gandhi referred to an analogous unified process as "education by the craft," insisting that education arises from life itself—through doing what one must, in order to survive. For Gandhi, this meant craft work, which would then serve the child, the family, and the community as an economic resource. Unlike the busy work prescribed in schools, the craft is not a mere exercise detached from life, but a vital means of participating in the life of the community. Similarly, for the deschooler, curriculum emerges from the relationship of the learner with others, and with the natural world.

Freedom: We ought to define conscientiously what we mean by "freedom." Freedom means much more than leaving kids alone; as social beings, we cannot be free without the love and support of others. Freedom requires the individual's conscious participation in the self-generative process of creating society, a collective undertaking in which the individual recognizes his or her duty to others, as well as a right to individuality. In Bakunin's words, "I can feel free only in the presence of and in relationship with other men (sic). . . . I am not myself free or human unless I recognize the freedom and humanity of all my fellow men."

As recognized members of this communal endeavor, children become responsible for the well-being of one another—an awareness of duty which thereby contributes to their own personal freedom. For the radical educator A. S. Neill, this is quite simply "freedom, not licence." To be free as a member of a community, one must respect the freedom of others. Deschoolers recognize that a child's development thrives upon this kind of freedom.

Society as a creative, communal effort: By encouraging questioning and rethinking, discussion and debate, exploration and discovery, disagreement and dissent—practices which lead to disequilibrium and, in turn, growth—deschooling requires us to face profound ambiguities. In turn, it allows us to recognize that society is a human creation—that it has no ultimate, articulate basis to which we can appeal, other than our own interdependency, and our powers of thought and imagination. This awareness frees us, and our children, to work toward transforming society as it stands.

Caring for children as a political activity: Since deschooling aspires to develop not only the free individual, but ultimately a free society, let's locate our description of this potential society in the framework of a body of political thought. It's democratic, in the actual sense of self-managed; and it's communal, taking root and developing within the local community. It derives from a long history of largely anarchist practice and from the ideals of social ecology. And it depends, ultimately, not on perfect and steadfast harmony, but on constant public scrutiny, open evaluation and re-evaluation, discussion, collective restructuring. Community members engage in regular dialogue in order to arrive at joint decisions and plans of action. Their concern is, of course, with the final outcome, but they are always deeply aware of the process through which they, as conscious members of a group, make changes in their own lives and social circumstances, recognizing their own communal interdependence, and their interdependence with the natural world. Since the form of such a society is regularly put into question, this activity is profoundly creative. It is also plainly analogous to the activity of deschooling.

This image, in fact, is what a community might look like, if it were to embrace the ideas of deschooling. In the ongoing attempt to restructure family life, tentative steps are currently being taken toward such a society; for instance, many families are rejecting the medicalization of birth, choosing their own homes as the ideal setting for the birth process, ensuring that control rests with the mother and child, not with a doctor. We can cite the growing popularity of a number of practices: holistic health care;

intentional communities and co-housing; childrearing philosophies emphasizing cooperation and intimacy over obedience and discipline; alternative family arrangements and shared childcare; and, of course, deschooling—choices which reject the combination of patriarchal authority, sexual repression, and professionalized indoctrination employed in conventional family organization, opting instead for a fuller, richer, more generous range of social possibilities. (We should point out that, as long as we allow ourselves to be intimidated by economic or social pressure to participate in the traditional institutions of marriage and the family, the prospects of "choice" in living and childrearing arrangements will remain blighted.)

Our role as parents and caregivers is not to ensure that our children develop the capacity to survive the rigors of modern life. Our task is to establish ways of childrearing so that children develop in a non-hierarchical relationship with others, and with the natural world—so that they genuinely regard freedom as education's ultimate end. We might even define deschooling as the development of a sensibility—nurturing a keen consciousness and appreciation of social and individual freedom, cultivating an unaffected capacity to imagine a communal, authentically democratic society with this image in mind, beginning with the creation and development of institutions such as freer, more humane, and more diverse alternatives to the family. With this definition, we embrace deschooling as a revolutionary opportunity.

9

Losing an Eye:
Some Thoughts on Real Safety

Matt Hern

Matt and his partner Selena operate a small community-based learning center for young deschooled kids. He is also working on a doctorate in Urban and Community Design, lectures at the Institute for Social Ecology, runs a small non-profit organization, and writes on a variety of subjects, including a weekly basketball column. He and Selena live with their daughter Sadie in the East End of Vancouver, British Columbia.

Matt wrote this in 1994, as part of a larger attempt to explain anarchist, egalitarian and deschooling theory in terms of specific, practical application. His further interest lies in deconstructing the myth that kids who grow up constantly monitored will somehow be "safe." This article expands our understanding of safety, and moves us towards trusting kids to be themselves.

I WAS SITTING ON A SWING, GENTLY MOVING BACK AND FORTH AND watching the kids tear around this park in our neighborhood. It's a nice park, a chunk of grass the size of a city block. It's got some decent play equipment in one corner, a bunch of huge oak trees, a bathroom and drinking fountain at one end and lots of well-kept turf. It's a good place for kids in an area that has lots of good places, and the small ones were having a great time.

I was being responsible and respectful, watching them carefully and trying not to get in the way of their game too often. I hadn't spoken to them for at least fifteen minutes and they were a good seventy yards away, frolicking. I couldn't help but wonder if they really needed me there. I thought back to when I was six or seven years old, and growing up in the country. I remembered taking off and roaming miles from home on my own. My brother and I would wander off down the beach, exploring, and not come back for hours. Yeah, I thought, but this is the nineties, not the seventies, and it's the city. And I wondered when these kids were going to get a chance to play away from constant adult surveillance and monitoring.

I tried to figure out how these kids could experience any real adventure, do any real exploring in this anaesthetized urban world. We live in a poor, downtown neighborhood in a big city, so there's a certain kind of adventuring to be done, but it's all within an adult context. There is little, if any, opportunity for young kids to take off on their own and investigate. The places "for kids" are just that, made for kids, by adults. I am a parent and run a small, deschooled learning center for elementary-aged kids, and am thus swamped with responsible adult concerns about safety in all its senses, and I am still left with the feeling that we adults have created a bland, over-monitored, dull and disabling world for our kids to play in—especially in the city.

I see a modern world that is safety-obsessed to the point that every facility in my neighborhood—parks, swimming pools, community centers, skating rinks, and everything else—is monitored and supervised enthusiastically by multi-levelled authority. I took a bunch of kids up a local mountain to play in the snow recently, and we parked the bus and found a steep hill to fling ourselves down. A ranger quickly scooted up in his jeep to tell us that we weren't allowed to slide down the hill: we had to use the designated "tobogganing area." I protested somewhat, and he disgustedly muttered, "Some people think they have the God-given right to kill themselves!"

I don't have any real interest in mythologizing childhoods of decades past, nor in romanticizing kids' ability to keep themselves safe, but when I can't even drive 40 minutes out of the city and slide down an empty hill without some guy in a uniform telling me where to go, I get a little troubled. If we want and expect our kids to grow up to be responsible creatures capable of directing their own lives, we have to give them practice at making decisions. To allow authority continually to rob our kids of basic decisions about where and how to play is to set our kids up for dependence and incompetence on a wide scale. Safety is always a dominating concern for everyone hanging out with kids, and the way to promote safety is to help our kids become stronger, not weaker. Surveillance and control ensures weakness; responsibility encourages strength.

Like all parents, I can't help but be confused and concerned by the constant stream of child abductions, killings, and rapes. I can't help but look at my daughter and want nothing to hurt her. I want to protect her—and at the same time I really want to stay out of her way. I really want her to have the space to make herself up. I think I understand what John Holt meant when, writing about reading, he said that kids "need stories of real danger, adventure, heroism, not just talk about what it's like to go with Mommy to the supermarket" (*Schooling at Home*, p.40). I think they need exploration and excitement in their lives as well, and this makes much sense and makes for a great paradox. How can we keep our kids safe in an insane and violent world, and still allow them the freedom to explore, to adventure and to create themselves outside of adult surveillance?

I am not prepared to answer that question simply with "get out of the city." Many of us live in the city for important and excellent reasons. And as Colin Ward wrote in *The Child in the City*, kids can flourish in cities and play a crucial role in humanizing urban environments. The thrust of Ward's book is a very useful analysis "about the ways in which the link between city and child can be made more fruitful and enjoyable for both the child and the city." I believe that there may be more opportunities for self-directed activity for kids outside of urban centers, and I believe that there are other answers as well. I am convinced that kids, when loosed from authoritarian control, are able to direct much of their lives safely and creatively. I believe that this assumption shifts the question from how adults can make activities more and more safe, to how adults can find ways to give kids more and more control over their lives.

I can envision a three-part approach to helping our kids become stronger and safer. A combination of egalitarian parenting, unschooling, and community participation may begin to answer a violent and crazy world with responsible kids and families. It is clearly possible to examine parenting seriously and to examine whether or not we are encouraging the development of self-directing, rather than dependent, humans. I believe a style of parenting is possible which encourages and nurtures the development of responsible kids, and I want to support approaches to parenting which are neither authoritarian nor permissive nor authoritative, but egalitarian.

Traditional thought about parenting has continually focused on ways in which parents can enforce their own agendas about what their children should be doing. If we as parents can learn to listen to our kids on many different levels and can trust our kids from the very beginning to make good and important decisions about what they do and don't want, we have made a start. Further, if we can learn to structure our language and behavior so as to support our kids' decisions, we can increase children's chances of success in creating themselves. And if they are confident and secure, kids will be far stronger and more capable of directing themselves.

Compulsory schooling clearly plays a major role in the undermining of our kids safety by undermining their ability to monitor and direct their own lives. For an overwhelming proportion of the natural youth of most kids, they are contained in bizarre institutions, herded around like sheep, and continually told what to do. For a minimum of twelve years, compulsory schooling refuses to allow kids the opportunity to make any important decisions about their own lives. As John Taylor Gatto writes, "School takes our children away from any possibility of an active role in community life. . . and by doing so ensures our children cannot grow up fully human." (*Dumbing Us Down*, p.14) With so little real practice, it is no wonder that so many kids have so much trouble making good choices. Kids who can make good decisions are going to be safer than those who can't, and schools do nothing to support that responsibility. Alternative settings, especially homelearning, must be considered as an important step in keeping our kids really safe.

Finally, I want to suggest community as a critical piece of this analysis. Living in a cohesive and supportive community can be a huge factor in ensuring the safety of everyone, especially children. By community I mean town, neighborhood, block, street, rural area—having people around us who know and care about our lives is another piece of keeping kids safe. Neighbors watching out the windows, people talking to each other on the street, friends knowing where kids live, folks sitting out on their porches and storekeepers waving, among countless other things, are all aspects of community that make our kids more secure. If children are living in a place where they can be comfortable, their opportunities for exploration are greatly increased. If kids can wander and play with many eyes watching out for them, without having to explicitly monitor them, genuine safety is possible.

What I am really looking for is a deprofessionalization of childcare. Over the past number of decades a liberal ethic of professionalism has swamped mainstream Western thought, and most people who spend time around kids believe they are required to justify their position with a pseudo-mystical, hierarchical authority. Professionalism is entirely different from competence in that professionals not only claim special knowledge of what is right, they usurp the ability to prescribe proper action for their "clients." Ivan Illich writes:

> Professionals tell you what you need and claim the power to prescribe. They not only recommend what is good, but actually ordain what is right. . . . This professional authority comprises three roles: the sapiential authority to advise, instruct and direct; the moral authority that makes its acceptance not just useful but obligatory; and charismatic authority that allows the professional to appeal to some supreme interest of his client that not only outranks conscience but sometimes even the *raison d'etat.*

This ethic has infused current Western thought so deeply that parents, in addition to teachers and instructors and coaches and day care workers and everyone else, believe that professional authority is the key to their effectiveness and appropriatenes in dealing with kids.

If kids are to be genuinely safe, this ethic must be deconstructed. If we are interested in safety in the broadest sense, our kids have to make decisions, learn how to choose their activities, to assess danger, and to be in relationship. And that's the key. I want to suggest that deschooling is about relationships, and is the antithesis of professionalism. Genuine relationships are exactly what teachers are looking to avoid. It is what they call "unprofessional." But if adults are willing to take the time to get to know the kids they are around really well, to spend large amounts of time with their daughters and sons, to listen carefully to their needs and wants, and to understand what they are capable of, then trust can't be far behind. And if we can trust them to make important decisions, then the question of safety is one within the context of relationship and caring, and removed from professional service and petty authority.

This seems to be the start of an answer. Constant surveillance and monitoring is not the path to real safety for our kids. In trusting children to make decisions about their lives, we can support the development of responsibility at many levels. If kids can be treated with egalitarian intent at home, be allowed to run their days free from schooled control, and can live in genuine community, then happy, self-directing kids and real safety are genuinely within reach.

10

Learning? Yes, of course.
Education? No, thanks.

Aaron Falbel

Aaron Falbel is a free-lance writer, editor, philosopher, and musician. Together with Gene Burkart, and under the guidance of Ivan Illich, he is attempting to piece together the history of homo educandus. *He lives with his wife Susannah Sheffer in Cambridge, Massachusetts.*

This article, originally printed in the magazine, Growing Without Schooling *(#92), presents a cogent analysis of education. Aaron is a careful and clear thinker, and this piece reflects his thorough understanding of both Holt and Illich. His analysis and suggestions are radical, but also practical and reasonable.*

IN 1982, A BRITISH INTERVIEWER ASKED JOHN HOLT HOW HE DEFINED the word "education." He responded: "It's not a word I personally use. . . . The word "education" is a word much used, and different people mean different things by it. But on the whole, it seems to me what most people mean by "education" has got some ideas built into it or contains certain assumptions, and one of them is that learning is an activity which is separate from the rest of life and done best of all when we are not doing anything else, and best of all where nothing else is done—learning places, places especially constructed for learning. Another assumption is that education is a designed process in which some people do things to other people or get other people to do things which will presumably be for their own good. Education means that some A is doing something to somebody else B. I guess that, basically, is what most people understand education to be about."

The interviewer pressed John further: "Very well, but what is your definition?"

John replied, "I don't know of any definition of it that would seem to me to be acceptable. I wrote a book called *Instead of Education*, and what I mean by this [title] is instead of this designed process which is carried on in specially constructed places under various kinds of bribe and threat. I don't know what single word I'd put [in its place]. I would talk about a process in which we become more informed, intelligent, curious, competent, skillful, aware by our interaction with the world around us, because of the mainstream of life, so to speak. In other words, I learn a great deal, but I do it in the process of living, working, playing, being with friends. There is no division in my life between learning, work, play, etc. These things are all one. I don't have a word which I could easily put in the place of 'education,' unless it might be 'living.' "

I wrote the following statement at the request of Ivan Illich to try to explain the difference between learning and education. I realize that "education" is a difficult word to pin down—some people may use it in the way that I use the word "learning." But I believe that John Holt is right in saying that most people use "education" to refer to some kind of *treatment*. (Even "self-education" can reflect this: a self-administered treatment.) It is this usage that I am contrasting with learning, and this idea of people needing treatment, whether carried out in schools or homes or wherever, that I wish to call into question.

★

Many people use the words "learning" and "education" more or less interchangeably. But a moment's reflection reveals that they are not at all the same. I invite you to take this moment and reflect with me on this idea.

Learning is like breathing. It is a natural, human activity: it is part of being alive. A person who is active, curious, who explores the world using all his or her senses, who meets life with energy and enthusiasm—as all babies do—is *learning*. Our ability to learn, like our ability to breathe, does not need to be improved or tampered with. It is utter nonsense, not to mention deeply insulting, to say that people need to be taught how to learn or how to think. We are born knowing how to do these things. All that is needed is an interesting, accessible, intelligible world, and a chance to play a meaningful part in it.

If the air is polluted, then it can become difficult to breathe. We cough, wheeze, and gasp for air. Similarly, if our social environment is polluted, it can become difficult to learn. Today our social environment is thoroughly polluted by *education*—a designed process in which one group of people (educators, social engineers, people shapers) tries to make another group (those who are to be "educated") learn something, usually without their consent, because they (the "educators") think it will be good for them. In other words, education is forced, seduced or coerced learning—except that you can't really make another person learn something that he or she doesn't want to learn, which is why education doesn't work *and has never worked*. People have always learned things, but *education* is a relatively recent innovation, and a deeply destructive one at that.

It is ironic that education, carried out by well-meaning people hoping to produce or enhance learning, ends up attacking learning. But this is precisely what happens, despite all the good intentions. In the climate of education, learning is cut off and disembedded from active life. It is divorced from personal curiosity and is thus profoundly denatured. Learning shrivels as it becomes the result of a process controlled, manipulated and governed by others. It deteriorates into empty actions done under the presure of bribe and threat, greed and fear. We all know this to be true from our own "educational" experiences.

When I speak of education, I am not referring only to that which goes on in schools. Today "education" takes place in many guises and settings: through the mass media, in the workplace, and in the home. We adopt the *educative stance* when we feel it is our right and duty to manipulate others for their own good.

Let me be clear: I am not against all forms of teaching. It is a privilege and a joy to help someone do something he or she has freely chosen to do, provided that we are invited to help. I am against unasked-for, I'm-doing-this-for-your-own-good teaching.

I do have a problem with *professional* teachers—people who try to turn whatever knowledge they might have into capital, into a commodity. I want to live in a society where casual, asked-for teaching is a matter of courtesy, not a quick way to make a buck. Sure, there are times when it is proper to compensate a teacher for his or her time and effort. But the new educational supermarkets, which offer courses (for a fee) on everything from breastfeeding to sensitivity training are a step in the wrong direction. Though such courses are not compulsory, they end up convincing people that learning through living is inferior to instruction. For instance, why learn to diaper a baby by watching Granny do it when you can receive "parental education" from a professional parental instructor?

Most of us have forgotten what it was like to follow our own noses, to ask our own questions and find our own answers. Years of educational treatment have convinced us that learning is, and can only be, the result of teaching. We grow up into adults who insist that our children "receive" an education. We trust neither ourselves nor our children to learn.

The last thing I want to do is *improve* education: rather I want to escape its noxious fumes, to offer my help to anyone seeking similar detoxification, and to clean up the environment where I can. If you are interested in joining me, there are some steps that you and I can take that will help clear the air of "education" and create a cleaner social environment supportive of learning.

First, let us rid our own minds of the prejudice that views others who opt out of educational treatment as "delinquents," "failures," or "dropouts." Let us view them instead as wise *refuseniks*, as conscientious objectors to a crippling and dehumanizing process. Let us act in a way that removes the stigma currently hanging over the heads of educational underconsumers.

Second, if we agree that children are good at learning, let our attitude and dealings with young people bear this out. Let us resist the temptation to become educators, to rub the noses of the young in our greater experience by adopting the roles of teacher, helper, and instructor at the drop of a hat. Let us trust people to figure things out for themselves, *unless* they specifically ask for our help. (As it turns out, they ask frequently. Small children, whose curiosity has not been deadened by education, are usually brimming over with questions.) The nature of the toxicity inherent in education is precisely that so much of the teaching that goes on is unasked for. Let us endeavor to rid our own behavior of unasked-for help.

Third, let us not discriminate against the uncertified when it comes to the matter of employment. Several landmark studies have shown that there is no correlation between educational training and performance on the job. (See especially Ivar Berg's *The*

Great Training Robbery, Beacon Press, 1971.) If we must assess competence for a given job, let us assess it as directly as we can, and not conflate competence with length of sitting done in educational institutions. We can also deflate the value of educational currency by refusing to talk about our own educational credentials. Take them off your resumé! Demand that others judge you by your actual talents and accomplishments, as you would judge others.

Fourth, let us do our own part to create a more open and accessible society, where knowledge and tools are not locked up in institutions or hoarded as closely guarded secrets, by offering (not imposing) to share our skills with others. Take on an apprentice. Hang a shingle outside your home describing what you do. Let your friends and neighbors know that you are making such an offer to any serious and committed person.

Fifth, let us outlaw *exploitative* labor, not child labor, the prohibition of which currently denies many forms of meaningful participation to the young. This will help end the policy of age discrimination, which mandates that the young be taught *about* the world before they are allowed to learn *from* it by participating *in* it.

Sixth, let us support libraries, museums, theatres, and other voluntary, non-coercive community institutions. (Many libraries, for example, are open only during working hours, when only those with the luxury of a research stipend may use them. With more support, they could be open evenings and weekends.) Additionally, let us create more spaces in our communities where young and old (and those in between), can get together to pursue unprogrammed activities of all sorts: arts, crafts, sports, music, hobbies, discussion groups, etc. Let us end the policy of shunting young and old into separate institutions "for their own good."

Finally, think up more ideas of your own! As a society that has been addicted to education for several generations, we have lost the ability to imagine what it might be like to grow up and live in a world free of pedagogical manipulation.

If you agree with this statement, or just find it provocative, make copies and discuss it with your family, friends, neighbors, and fellow workers. Send a copy to distant friends and invite them to do the same.

Anne Franklin

Part Three — Just Say No: Staying Home

11

Dinosaur Homeschool

Donna Nichols-White

Donna Nichols-White is the mother of three homeschooled children, editor and publisher of The Drinking Gourd, Multicultural Home Education Magazine, *and the owner and operator of* The Drinking Gourd Book Company *which offers books, software, and lab equipment geared towards independent learning.*

This article directly addresses the myth that deschooling or homeschooling is only available to middle- and upper-class white families. "Dinosaur Homeshool" is a clear view of the often complicated and confusing process of having kids stay at home. Donna's vision and energy are obvious, as is her pride in her family.

IT'S TUESDAY AFTERNOON, THE HOUSE IS QUIET, THE NEIGHBORHOOD children are in school. I calmly settle down to eat lunch. Suddenly, I am alerted by a strange sound—whrrr, whrrr, whrrr...

I look across the table, startled. A dinosaur is lumbering towards me. I am astonished. A real dinosaur? I thought that they either never existed or were extinct.

This dinosaur is certainly real. It is about 8" high, has four legs and a long tail. He looks different from the dinosaurs I have seen in books because he is connected to several wires, has eyes that light up and makes a strange whirring noise.

I chuckle to myself. I know this dinosaur is being tested, will soon be interfaced with a computer, programmed to light up, go forwards or backwards, and make noise.

Khahil, age nine, Latif, age seven, and Rukiya, age three, are at it again. They have built a dinosaur with a toy construction set.

I chuckle while saying to myself, "And people wonder why I

homeschool."

I have always had my children home with me. When the boys were young I was considered an extinct or non-existent species myself, "the black housewife." Clifford and I struggled financially on his income in order that I might stay home. I thought raising babies and toddlers was one of the most enjoyable jobs that I could have.

By the time my eldest was four, I knew that I would homeschool my children. My sons were not going to become stereotypical "endangered black males." I planned for them to become intelligent, independent, and productive men.

Rarely is information about black families who homeschool offered. Three years ago I embarked upon a mission to find families like ours. So far I have been either contacted by, or informed of, over three hundred black homeschooling families throughout the United States, Canada, and the Virgin Islands. I'm sure this is only a small sample because I've discovered many of us prefer to remain anonymous; many black parents think that if school authorities discover how readily and willingly we'll remove our children from school, they will design laws to force us to bring them back.

Black homeschoolers tend to view institutionalized education as a form of slavery. And they fear the government will enact truancy laws, like the fugitive slave laws, more often upon black families than white families.

The dinosaur is still heading towards me. He is the sum total of four hours' worth of direction following. Instead of reading, writing, show and tell, arithmetic, etc., Khahil and Latif have been playing with their building toys. During this play they have learned physics, electronics, multi-step direction following, team work, cooperation, computing and programming—not to mention how to deal with a three-year-old sister while doing all of these things. There isn't a textbook in sight and they're learning in spite of this so-called deprivation.

You see, long ago I decided I would not imitate school. I would teach phonics, reading, and math skills, but I wouldn't spend six hours a day, five days a week on those subjects. I thought that would be inefficient and a complete waste of time.

How do I know my children are faring well academically?

When was the last time you met a seven-year-old who not only built dinosaurs but computer-controlled them? Are basal reading materials more productive?

In the United States a foreign-born person who learns English as a second language has a better chance of becoming literate than a native born Black American (most of whom were schooled). A concerned homeschool parent has a better chance of teaching their child to read than the schools do.

Is making good grades and passing tests a guarantee of a job in the future? Not by today's standards. The ability to think, be flexible, master more than one language, and possess computer literacy are the present job qualifications. How many black children are being taught these skills? If indeed they can be taught.

"What about the cost? Black parents can't afford to homeschool."

In the past three years I have met single parents, adoptive parents, welfare parents, and families who lived well below the poverty level who homeschooled their children. I know teenagers who homeschooled themselves responsibly while their parents worked.

"Well, you can afford a computer-controlled building set but most black families can't."

This is a funny one. Usually the folks who tell me this have supplied their children with the latest video game equipment. My children feel deprived because we won't buy video games; instead, we've spent the same amount of money on computer-controlled building toys.

During slavery, the white folks got the ham, while we had to live off the chitlins. The same conditions exist today. The best in education goes to rich children and we are receiving the scraps (regardless of how great our school district is). Well, scraps will not make our children independent.

I consider video games the scraps. Children sit staring like morons at a screen while controlling visual pictures with a joystick, button, glove, etc. They are learning how to sit, stare at a screen, and push buttons all day long. They are not learning how to use today's technology as a tool. Most important, they are not learning how to build, create, and think.

"Most parents aren't qualified to homeschool their children."

Do you think that I know how to program a dinosaur? No, I've already stated the fact that native-born black Americans are more likely to be illiterate than foreign born peoples. Come on, we native-born black people have been attending schools for years. It doesn't take that long to teach a child to read, write, etc. Besides, our goal should be independent, self-directed learning—a goal rarely achieved through schooling.

"But what about socialization?"

Homeschoolers tire of this question. It reminds me of what my mother told me as a child, "I didn't send you to school to socialize, I sent you there to get an education." Since when does the black community think more highly of socialization than education? I remember trying to encourage two economically well-off adult black men to build a hotel and convention center. Their response, "We can't do that yet because we have to start getting together first." I hope my children will grow up to be producers, not party goers who feel the need to bond socially instead of economically.

After my daughter was born I started an at-home business. In addition to homeschooling I work about 60 hours a week—at home. I work with my children in tow. Having received no business (self-employment) education myself, I've decided to learn my business, through trial and error, failure and success, within full view of my children. I'm showing them that families can work and learn together.

The dinosaur is ready to be hooked to the computer and programmed. I'm anxious to see if the experiment works, so I follow my children.

As my children continue to build and program, read and write, I operate my business. Like hundreds of black families nationwide, we are home, they are homeschooled, and our family thrives.

12

Family Matters:
Why Homeschooling Makes Sense

David Guterson

David Guterson is a former high school English teacher and a writer whose first collection of short stories The Country Ahead Of Us, The Country Behind, *was published in 1989 and whose nonfiction has been published in* Harper's Magazine. *He lives with his wife, three sons, and newborn daughter on Bainbridge Island, Washington.*

This piece is excerpted from the book of the same name which, since its publication in 1992, has proved both popular and useful. For many years, Guterson was a high school English teacher and a homeschooling parent, a vantage point which allowed him to view the absurdities, incongruities, and contradictions of modern educational thought.

A S A PUBLIC-SCHOOL TEACHER AND A HOMESCHOOLING PARENT, I find myself moving between two worlds almost on a daily basis. School is the world of the fixed curriculum, an inert body of knowledge and skills to be disseminated on a fixed schedule. Its content is ultimately in the hands of professionals who have acquainted themselves with state and district guidelines and who exert themselves to stay in touch with the needs of the nation and community. They must also take into account the immense complications of large scale schooling and adapt both curricula and methods to it so that the content of education can in fact be transmitted, or at least partially transmitted, against the odds. Thus the schedule of the day and year is made routine, because no other timetable lends itself to an institution of such unwieldy proportions, and content is tailored to a sense of what the group needs rather than the individual. Creativity is limited by the sheer size of the student population and by the individual teacher's resolute commitment to meet the needs of the many, to commit to one method that has limited effectiveness but is at the same time the lesser of many evils. School is about delivering instruction, learner outcomes, mastery of content, and feedback with correction. It is in many ways an abstraction and ultimately a weariness of the spirit. Children, in the majority of cases, adapt to it against their wills.

Proponents of the school-of-hard-knocks approach will reply that this process of reluctant adaptation is a fine and necessary part of education and teaches young people the truth about adult life. Expect to be misunderstood; expect to be bored by much of what comes your way; expect to be ignored, to have your needs go unmet, to have to adjust to the world—don't expect it to adjust to you. They are right, of course, that these lessons must be learned and that schools teach these lessons exceedingly well, with great power, perhaps indelibly. The sad part is that in the process schools have also been exceedingly good at snuffing out the desire of many young people to understand their world. Schools have taught them to associate learning with this painful form of misunderstanding and with a frustrated boredom that ought to be the exception in their educational experience, not the rule. To acclimate students to misery under the rubric that so doing prepares them for life is a cynical notion—and a horrifying one. Rather, in shaping the academic experiences of our young, we should recall that they are individuals who, with no help from our institutions—but because life simply is what it is—will learn by osmosis of the injustice of the adult world they will one day both define and inhabit.

Some schools have grudgingly and painfully come to terms with themselves but only in the face of mounting failures. Many now recognize that sooner or later they must confront the existence of individual learning styles and adapt to their reality. One response has been the adoption of "mastery learning" programmes, which break down a long series of educational objectives into incremental and sequential modest goals. Imagine a child seated alone, systematically making her way through a geography workbook, and you are imagining, in essence, mastery learning. Students master each humble step methodically, moving toward unit tests that are corrected and returned to them as "feedback." The idea here is to allow for a variety of learning rates without giving up the notion of a schoolwide curriculum. Students all continue to learn the same things; they simply learn them at rates better suited to their individual abilities.

Mastery learning has not been a panacea, though, chiefly because individual teachers are hugely overburdened by the daily task of administrating its details for such large numbers of students. (I have tried it myself. Thirty workbooks. Thirty students travelling at different rates through them, clamoring for attention when they stumble. Three are taking unit tests. Two are on page four of Book One, four are ripping through Book Three, five are bogged down in the middle of Book Two. I am trotting from the raised hand in row one to the raised hand in row four when the bell suddenly rings.) Mastery learning has, too, a pair of fatally flawed premises: that children learn best when the world is deconstructed into endless small components, and the method is ascendant over content (so the uniform subject matter of the workbooks is never called into question). Teachers who commit themselves to the concept and employ it in their classroom see very little transference of learning from the system's workbooks and progressive tests to the student's larger frame of reference. They find, ironically, that what their students have in fact "mastered"—if they master anything—is not some desired set of knowledge and skills but rather the mastery learning system itself and strategies required to confront it: reading between the lines of a workbook, for example, or filling in blanks with force-fed terms or ruling out deceptive multiple-choice options of a series of predictable examinations.

Progressive homeschoolers are apt to see mastery learning as a marked improvement over the strategies that preceded it, but it is still not very useful. Many are dedicated to the proposition that real learning takes place in the world beyond institutions and that no "instructional delivery system" can begin to approach the instruction delivered by life itself. They see the content of education—the knowledge and skills an education develops—as emerging out of experience in the world and not out of classrooms and workbooks. Grounded by reading or inclination in the educational theories of Jean Jacques Rousseau—who believed that young people develop best when adults refrain from imposing on them—these homeschoolers seek an education for their children free from coercion and control. "What children need," wrote John

Holt, a leading voice among progressive homeschoolers, "is not new and better curricula but access to more and more of the real world; plenty of time and space to think over their experiences, and to use fantasy and play to make meaning out of them; and advice, road maps, guidebooks, to make it easier for them to get where they want to go (not where we think they ought to go), and to find out what they want to find out."

But rigid or flexible, progressive or traditional, true education always begins with the child and with an understanding of her individual needs. The choice to put before her a fixed curriculum or a mastery learning program, or to nurture "access to more and more of the real world," is a function of the child's unique requirements as a learner. No curriculum or method is "best," and no philosophical premise about education supreme or universally applicable. Endless diversity is called for in the face of the endless diversity of children. Our methods and curricula are implied by who the children are and by what they individually need.

This diversity cannot be adequately addressed by schools as they currently operate, nor can it be addressed by homeschooling parents so thoroughly entrenched in their philosophical notions that their theories obscure the needs of their children. Abstractions about what works universally in education are best made secondary to the real needs of each child, while knowledge about what nurtures each should be acted on by those in a position to do so ably—whether they be teachers or parents or both together. The principle I suggest has a name among educators: child-centered education. It has come to mean a lot of things, but the term ought principally to remind us of our duty to shape the how and what of education not around a kernel of philosophical abstraction but around the needs of each unique child.

So while we might agree with those who believe that there is a set of things people need to know in order to be culturally literate (if not about what goes in that set), we should also resist the notion of a universal method to arrive there and insist that this literacy not be achieved at the expense of each child's love of learning. A belief in the importance of cultural literacy, in other words, should not prevent us from taking child-centered education seriously, for child-centered does not imply that each child should simply go her own way in pursuit of a self-absorbed curriculum. It does imply, on the other hand, that children in particular and families in general should exercise primary control over content, and it also implies a general faith in the far-reaching curiosity and inquisitiveness of young people. While such faith may not come easily to proponents of a national curriculum, it in fact paves the way for each child to grasp matters of importance with a depth and breadth far superior to the *Dictionary of Cultural Literacy*. Placing the child at the center of her education does not put our culture, by extension, on the periphery; on the contrary, it lays the groundwork for successfully bringing the two together, for instilling in her a lifelong thirst for understanding her world.

Child-centered education puts into perspective, too, the debate about when children should start learning. Progressive homeschoolers characterize this debate as irrelevant: children, they point out, are learning all the time, are learning even as they grow in the womb, thus the question about "beginning" at four or six or eight is for them a meaningless one. Opposite them stand advocates of intensive preschooling who espouse formal academic training for toddlers and even conscious attempts on the part of parents to educate their infants. Researchers, meanwhile, have made massive efforts to determine the proper age for initiating education and have come up with a variety of answers. Ultimately, burdened by the weight of endless administrative considerations, our schools go on operating under the assumption that at age six—the first grade—the formal education of all children should begin.

The child-centered response to this is obvious. Homeschoolers need not concern themselves with the one best age to begin an education—as researchers have and as schools must—but rather with the needs and interest of the individual child. We begin when they are ready—neither before nor after. This demands an intimate awareness on our part, an awareness that comes quite naturally to parents but to almost nobody else.

Educators in the past ten years have become increasingly fond of the term child-centered in discussing school reform. What many have failed to recognize is that the public-school teacher is in no position to place most children at or even near the center of their own learning. Even the most committed teacher, overwhelmed by sheer numbers and by the structure of school itself, must fail to arrive at the profound understanding of each child that is a prerequisite to his or her success. It is parents who possess this profound understanding and who are well positioned to act on it.

13

Doing Something Very Different: Growing Without Schooling

Susannah Sheffer

Susannah Sheffer is the author of several books, including A Life Worth Living: Selected Letters of John Holt, Writing Because We Love to: Homeschoolers at Work, *and* A Sense of Self: Listening to Homeschooled Adolescent Girls.

As the editor of Growing Without Schooling, *Susannah comes into contact with an immense number of homeschoolers, and this piece demonstrates how John Holt's ideas are being lived every day by unschooled kids. Much of Holt's particular genius lay in the easy faith he had in people's ability to do things for themselves, and Susannah has a clear understanding of both his intent and its implications.*

I'M SITTING WITH THREE TEENAGERS WHO HAVE RECENTLY LEFT SCHOOL to begin learning at home and in the wider world. On the table in front of us lie notes about possibilities—ideas, wishes, plans for further investigation. I've scribbled down, "Call homeless shelter; find out about marine biologist," in response to Anna's brainstorm of things she would like to do or learn more about. Adrienne and I have agreed to meet next week to talk about the essay she is working on. Ariel says that she wants to work with someone who can help her see what it means to think mathematically, rather than just how to complete math assignments, and I've recommended someone for her to call.

Though these kids have been homeschooling for a few months, they are still becoming accustomed to the freedom, to the heady realization that education can be about figuring out how to meet demands that don't make sense to them. I am struck again and again by their enthusiasm, their interest in learning, the number of things they come up with when they are asked what they want to know more about.

As we scrape the last crumbs of chocolate cake from our plates, our conversation turns toward their friends who are still in school and who are more often than not unhappy there. They say they want to let these kids know that homeschooling is an option for them. Speaking for the many skeptics, I offer a common criticism of homeschooling: "Some people might say that you are special kids, though, and that homeschooling can only work for kids who are as self-motivated as you are. After all, think of all the interests you've been telling me about..."

"But I wasn't like this at all last year!" Ariel interjects. "I wasn't the kind of kid you would think would be self-motivated. I didn't do that well in school, and I didn't have all these things I wanted to learn about."

The others agree. "Oh yeah," one says, "if you had to go by how I acted in school..."

"It's not fair to look at kids in school and say, oh, they're not motivated, oh, they're not good at this," someone else adds, "because maybe they would be a lot more motivated under a different system. The thing about homeschooling is that it's so different. I wish people could understand that."

"Why didn't school work for you?" I ask.

"No one was paying attention to what I really needed," Adrienne says. "And it was really hard for me to take myself seriously there. I was always doubting myself."

"It's hard to fit in there, but you have to fit in," Ariel adds. "School pits kids against each other."

"And you're cooped up all day, under those lights," Anna says. "It felt like we were being punished, that's what I always used to feel, like we were in there as a punishment."

Some people would call this adolescent griping. Why do I listen to these kids, this growing crop of new homeschoolers and their companions, the long-time homeschoolers who have learned outside of school for years, and feel that they are some of the most important education critics of our time? Why do I feel that these are the voices the school reform movement needs to hear?

John Holt wrote in 1970, "Every day's headlines show more clearly that the old ways, the tried and true ways, are simply and quite spectacularly not working. No point in arguing about who's to blame. The time has come to do something very different."[1] Homeschooling is about doing something very different. It's about making things better for kids right now, and at the same time it gives us a vantage point from which to look at the experience of kids in school and at the structure and assumptions of traditional schooling. These homeschoolers are worth listening to because they don't let us rest on old assumptions, because they are exuberant, full of interests, eager to learn—and they weren't like this in school a year ago. Something is different. That difference is what school reformers need to study.

Holt published the first issue of *Growing Without Schooling* *(GWS)* in 1977 as a way of supporting the families scattered across the country who were letting their children learn outside of school. Holt had been a teacher for many years, and his *How Children Fail* and several subsequent books had placed him at the center of the school reform movement of the 1960s and 70s. By the early 1970s he was questioning the idea of schooling itself. In the first issue of GWS, he wrote that the newsletter would be:

> about ways in which people, young and old, can learn to do things, acquire skills, and find interesting and useful work without having to go through the process of schooling. In starting this newsletter, we are putting into practice a nickel-and-dime theory about social change, which is that important and lasting change always comes slowly, and only when people change their lives, not just their political beliefs or parties.[2]

Growing Without Schooling, as Holt said elsewhere in that first issue, was "to make people feel less helpless," because it would show them that people could change things for themselves, could create new solutions in their own lives without waiting for an entire revolution to occur. Of course, the changes they did make would then be inspiring to others and would demonstrate that "something very different" was indeed possible.

Eighteen years later, many of the children who were babies when *GWS* was first launched have spent their entire lives reading, thinking, playing, studying, working with adults in the community, learning all manner of things, all without going to school. They have learned to read without traditional reading instruction, made friends even though most people think making friends without attending school is impossible, got into selective colleges (ditto), and found interesting work (ditto). John Holt published a book about homeschooling, called *Teach Your Own*, in 1981, and continued to publish *GWS* and learn from homeschoolers until his death in 1985. Holt Associates carries on with his work, publishing *GWS*, running a mail-order book catalogue, writing and speaking to and about homeschoolers.

In continuing John Holt's work, we are focused on the immediate needs of homeschoolers, but we also keep a broader or more long term vision in our minds. By helping people envision certain kinds of possibilities and put certain ideas into practice, we are also working to show what a very different kind of world might look like. In time, this actually helps to make our current world look a little more like that other, different one.

In Holt's *Freedom and Beyond*, which was first published in 1972, he wrote:

> Imagine that I am traveling into the future in a time capsule, and that I come to rest, five hundred years from now, in an intelligent, humane, and life-enhancing civilization. One of the people who lives there comes to meet me, to guide me, and to explain his society. At some point, after he has shown me where people live, work, play, I ask him,
>
> "But where are your schools?"
>
> "Schools? What are schools?" he replies.
>
> "Schools are where people go to learn things."
>
> "I do not understand," he says, "People learn things everywhere, in all places."
>
> "I know that," I say, "But a school is a special place where there are special people who teach you things, help you learn things."
>
> "I am sorry, but I still do not understand. Everyone helps other people to learn things. Anyone who knows something or can do something can help someone else who wants to learn more about it. Why should there be special people to do it?"
>
> And try as I will, I cannot make clear to him why we think that education should be, must be, separate from the rest of life.
>
> This was my first vision of a society without schooling. Since then I have come to feel that the deschooled society, a society in which learning is not separated from but joined to, part of the rest of life, is not a luxury for which we can wait hundreds of years, but something toward which we must move and work, as quickly as possible.[3]

This parable of Holt's is developed within the context of a much deeper and more detailed analysis of the function of schooling in society than I can give here. The story is useful, though, because it gives a vivid picture of what we are aiming for. It invites us to think about what stands between our current assumptions and those of that mythical future guide.

When I think about Holt's conversation with that tour guide, I think about the guide's bewilderment, his lack of comprehension. Though of course I feel myself to be trying to increase people's understanding, I'm also working toward a time when many of the things we now do to children and many of the ways we now think about children's learning simply won't make any sense.

The tour guide didn't understand what Holt meant when he said that schools are places where we go to learn things, and many of the long-time homeschoolers I know don't understand this either. Well, of course they understand it on some level, because it is an idea that permeates their culture, but they don't really understand it because they do *learn* everywhere, from everyone— at home, curled up on the couch reading or being read to, building or cooking or drawing or playing music or writing or having a conversation, and in libraries, museums, labs, courthouses, specialty shops, veterinary offices, theatres, newspapers, soup kitchens, historic houses, farms, wildlife sanctuaries—the list goes on, and these are all real examples of places homeschoolers visit and work as volunteers.

Naturally, as homeschoolers grow, they may find that they want to learn about or work on something in particular. They may decide that they want help in doing that. Homeschoolers understand the value of teachers, but they are less likely to understand why it's necessary to learn from people who are *only* teachers and/or to learn only from those teachers who are assigned to them. Homeschooling kids can ask for help, feedback, suggestions, inspiration, and support, and they and their families can create for themselves, as needed, whatever degree of schedule, planning, outside appointments, and deadlines they find useful. These families demonstrate what it means to create a useful structure rather than to labor under an externally imposed one. Homeschooling is important because of what it rejects, but it is equally (or perhaps more) important for what it reclaims on its own terms. Teachers, help, schedules, organization—these are not school things in themselves. They are school things when someone assigns the teachers, tells the teachers what to teach, gives the students no say in the matter, makes the help be compulsory, imposes the schedule according to institutional rather than individual needs, and so on. But when the teachers are chosen freely, the help is requested (and can be refused), and the schedules and organization serve real needs or goals, then these concepts mean something quite different.

Holt's tour guide wouldn't understand the need for grades and other external motivators, either. In a world where everyone learns all the time, people are learning on their own steam, for their own reasons, and they don't need the promise or threat of grades to make them learn or to tell them how well they did. *Growing Without Schooling* asked homeschooling kids and teenagers to describe situations in which they had to do something difficult or frustrating as part of working towards a larger goal.[4] "The pronunciation is difficult," a 15-year-old homeschooler wrote about her efforts to learn Spanish, but she kept practising because she really wanted to learn the language. "Although it would have been easy to quit, I decided not to," a 13-year-old wrote about his determination to remain on a challenging swim team because of his ambition to become a lifeguard. And after describing how hard she had to work to learn to sight read music, a 16-year-old lifelong homeschooler said, "I do things that are difficult, or that I really don't like, for the same reason I do anything else: because I've decided they're important." This is what our tour guide would understand but what so many schools fail to appreciate. Young people are capable of deciding what is important or necessary, and *once they have decided*, they are capable of working much harder than we imagine. Schools, after failing to give children the chance to decide what is important to them and to understand the relationship between their chosen goal and specific tasks, then conclude that children are lazy, no good, unmotivated. Proving this charge wrong is a large part of the work of *Growing Without Schooling*.

One of the consequences of thinking that people learn only in schools is that the culture ties up more of its resources in schools than in libraries, museums, public art facilities, community centers, and other places that are accessible but not compulsory and not restricted to one age group. Another part of our work at Holt Associates/*GWS*, though a less obvious part, is to support these existing community resources and to encourage development of new ones.

Holt's tour guide wouldn't judge people on the basis of how much time they've spent in schools. Unfortunately, we do judge people on that basis in our culture, but here again homeschoolers can be an exception and a suggestion of future possibilities. When homeschooling kids get into college, not on the basis of a high-school transcript but on the basis of what they have learned and done during those years, they show that there are other ways to evaluate people's abilities. When homeschoolers choose not to go to college but instead make their way into the adult world through apprenticeships and other interesting routes towards meaningful work, they show that college is not essential.

John Holt took an unusual approach to this problem of living in a culture that evaluates people according to school credentials. Having already acquired a couple of those credentials (though not as many as most people thought) before he developed his critique of schooling, he refused to include any mention of his schooling in public descriptions (on a book jacket, for instance, or on other occasions where such information is ordinarily given). Instead he said, "I have come to believe that a person's schooling is as much a part of his private business as his politics or religion, and that no one should be required to answer questions about it. May I say instead that most of what I know I did not learn in school, or even in what most people would call 'learning situations'."

John Holt's approach here is characteristic of his attitude toward social change in general. In a letter he wrote during the late 1970s he said,

> During the 1960s many young people were talking about revolutionary changes in society. Paul [Goodman] used to say to them, "Suppose you had had the revolution you are talking and dreaming about. Suppose your side had won, and you had the kind of society you wanted. How would you live, *you personally*, in that society? *Start living that way now!* Whatever you would do then, do it now. When you run up against obstacles, people or things that won't let you live that way, then begin to think about how to get over or around or under that obstacle, or how to push it out of the way, and your politics will be concrete and practical." Very good advice. The trick is to find ways to put your strongest ideals into practice *in daily life*. I don't mean talking to other people about it, or saying, "Wouldn't it be wonderful if we all did this or that." I mean doing it right now. It is interesting, absorbing, fascinating, satisfying, and useful. You don't have to wait for a

hundred million people to agree with you, you can start right away. And when you find that you are able to do something, the very fact that you can do it means that anyone else who wants to can also do it.[5]

This is what I try to do, what we try to do at Holt Associates, and what, in a sense, homeschoolers are doing as they simultaneously try to live in a way that makes sense and in so doing illuminates the possibilities for all of us. It's true that we are not anywhere near the kind of society that Holt's imagined tour guide lives in. But what would it look like? How would people live? What would no longer be true or necessary, and what would remain? Homeschooling is about figuring out answers to these questions and then—as Holt suggests—about trying to live as though those changes had already happened. Circuitous? Maybe. But it's the most direct route I know to the world where that tour guide lives.

Notes:

1. John Holt, *What Do I Do Monday?* New York: Dell Publishing Co., 1970, p. 302.
2. *Growing Without Schooling* #1, Vol. 1, No. 1, August 1977, p. 1.
3. John Holt, *Freedom and Beyond*. New York: Dell Publishing Co., p. 117.
4. "Working Toward a Goal," *Growing Without Schooling* #84, Vol. 14, No. 6, December 1991, pp. 14-17.
5. "Celebrating 100 Issues," *Growing Without Schooling* #100, Vol. 17, No. 3, July/August 1994, p. 35.

14

Thinking about Play, Practice, and the Deschooling of Music

Mark Douglas

Mark Douglas has been a prospector, cook, janitor, hitchhiker, musician, composer, artist, dad, and gardener, and has been giving music lessons for many years. In exchange for studio space in a learning center in Vancouver, he lets the kids play on his instruments and shares his understanding of music. Mark's range of knowledge, his clear understanding of deschooling, and his gentle ability to let kids proceed at their own rate is impressive. Asked to write about his experience, he produced the following piece in which practical advice illuminates his approach to music and deschooling.

HOW CAN YOU DESCHOOL MUSIC?
Stop thinking about music as a thing to learn and start thinking about it as a thing to do.

Despite academies and conservatories, methodologies and method books, pedagogies and pedagogues and millions of rapped knuckles, the active verb in relation to the word *music* is "to play." You *play* music. You can also *make* music. Playing and making are the essential elements in becoming a musician.

In becoming familiar with an instrument and how you can use it, you should play with it as much as possible. I *don't* mean practise it, I mean play with it. When you like, as often as you like or don't like, for as long or as little as you feel like it. In this way you find how playing and making music fits into your life and what kinds of sounds you enjoy producing.

Encourage playing and making as opposed to practising and

working on. If you practise you aren't really doing it. You are always in preparation for when you're really going to do it. Well, when are you really going to do it? At a lesson for your teacher? For adjudicators in an exam or judges in a competition? For parents or friends? Once you've really done it and your parent/teacher/judge lets you know whether you've succeeded in making music or not, are you ever going to really do it again?

Practising and performance go hand in hand with what has become our most common and most powerful concept regarding the purpose of music. This concept places an emphasis on the performance and the performer as the most important aspect of music. Performers (image) and performances (recording) are crucial in this concept because they are so eminently marketable and, increasingly, we are accepting the market as our ultimate judge. Within this frame of reference, the only real music is the stuff that passes this ultimate test.

No wonder practice becomes such a bogey to parents and kids alike. When you "perform" at a lesson or on request for relations and you haven't been practising and doing the work you know you should have been doing and you fail to perform up to everyone's expectations (real or imagined) including your own, you feel bad. You do not feel like a musician. You may feel like lying. You may dislike yourself and feel guilty. You may resent your teacher and parents for putting you through all this. You may feel all these things and you may feel them even more intensely because you were the one who *wanted* the lessons! Whatever you feel, I guarantee that you will not feel very musical.

Focus on performance, whether it be for your teacher or anyone else, can initiate a complex of feelings; guilt at being unprepared and anxiety about the coming "performance," frustration at doing poorly, resentment that it takes so much work to be "good," that it doesn't feel like fun at all, that your parents (or other people) are always reminding you to practise.

Ultimately, what's known as "resistance to practice" sets in. To a child, refusing to cooperate may feel like the only option available to her. It is an effort by the child to regain a sense of control of the experience of music, which by the time she reaches this stage, probably has not felt rewarding for some time. Eventually, persistent refusal usually elicits a conditional warning from a parent and/or teacher, "Better get down to work and show some commitment if you want to keep those lessons and that instrument..." If things go further, then lessons end and the instrument goes back to the store, is sold, or worse, sits there in the house, a silent but powerful testament to the child's failure and proof of their lack of any real musical ability.

When a youngster first expresses interest and enthusiasm for learning music, what happens in an adult mind? I wonder how differently we hear that request from what is meant by the child? I think it must sound very different to us and *mean* something very different to us than other requests that we deal with; can I have a chocolate bar? get a video? go camping? visit a friend? and so on. These are things we expect from a child and they are in fact *childish* requests. But the request to learn music or an instrument? This is a very *adult* thing. It may feel like the first indication from the child of something "serious" they wish to undertake, a first request that isn't some form of "play." So the request often gets taken seriously and serious results are expected because we know that music automatically means Lessons From A Teacher and a serious adult-sized Purchase Of An Instrument, not to mention Scheduling. After all, adults know (even if they aren't musicians themselves) how much hard work, dedication, and commitment is required to become a good musician. They also know how much it might cost.

Music is something that connects the adult world on a long, broad continuum to childhood. An interest in learning to play an instrument may seem like a tentative request to enter the adult world, a world of conditions and demands. "Look, if we're going to pay for these lessons, we want to see some progress." "If you stick to it and work really hard for a year we'll see about getting you your own instrument." "You've got to practise 30 minutes a day, or there's no birthday party on Saturday." "If you're going to be any good, you've got to work hard. I've got to work hard at my job and practising is your job, so go do it."

All this pressure flies in the face of the purpose of doing music: to make or be a more well-rounded person, to acquire another form of expression, for enjoyment and fun.

I think it is cruel to hold a six- or eight- or ten-year-old kid to adult terms of commitment when many adults do not themselves understand the meaning of the word. The many failures and tragedies that we adults have lived through and still carry with us cannot be healed by enforcing default regimens on the young around us. Music is to be enjoyed on its own terms, not because it fills another's agenda.

Currently, I make my living as a music teacher. From the beginning I've been suspicious of myself and in a state of watchfulness because I have no teacher training. This has led me to examine my students more from their point of view (boredom, resistance, and anxiety) than from a teacher's point of view (failing to measure up to what I know they must learn).

Eventually I decided not to be a teacher. Instead I try to create a relationship and environment in which students are free to explore a musical side to their creativity without my judgment. I only rely on teaching when I am at a complete loss, usually when I am too tired to listen and just to be there for the student. At such times I actually announce, "OK, I'm going to be a teacher now."

I have come to feel that a period of several years is consumed in exploring and experimenting with ways to make music before anything like technical "practice" can take place. The length of this period probably depends on many factors—the age of the child, how long they've been playing, their affinities, their home environment. I suspect that this period of experimentation lasts two to five years and ends approximately with the onset of puberty.

This period should be one of uncompromised and unjudged support. There should be no talk of long commitments, of conditional instrument acquisitions, or of when they will learn some real music. This type of conversation/pressure/expectation deal puts the endeavor under the control of someone other than the student, usually a parent, and then a new game has begun. The child will surely find ways to regain control of the experience and most of these ways produce anxiety for the parents. The original intent becomes subverted.

A child should never, under any circumstances, be forced to play—even if it seems like a waste of money to the parents. If a child knows he or she can ask to go to another teacher, change instruments or quit without guilt, then they will surely do so when they feel the arrangement is not giving them anything.

During the period when a child learns language, adults have no end of patience. Indeed, they expect that the child will produce numerous ineffective, idiosyncratic, and original attempts to communicate. Some of these may be memorable, humorous, irritating, or even disturbing, but we let them go because in the end we realize that the child will learn to talk.

I approach each student with the same faith that musical

language will result. I also consider that, given an unjudging environment, I have no idea what the nature of a particular person's expression may be. I try to make no assumptions. I do not know whether a child *needs* to know how to read standard notation. Maybe they will be better served by designing their own system for remembering their ideas. Maybe all their music will exist on tape or computer disk or in their heads. Maybe they need to learn how to play just one song well. Maybe they will be a composer. Most of the world's music is made by people who don't need a notation system and who haven't learned their music from a teacher in the same sense that we have.

The best way to learn music is to play it, play it, and make it with your family and friends.

15

Homeschooling as a Single Parent

Heather Knox

Heather Knox has worked as a childbirth education and labor support person in British Columbia, and is currently studying to be a homeopathic practitioner. In addition to working with homelearning families, she is the single parent of nine-year-old Megan. This article addresses directly the issue of being a single parent with a deschooled child, dispelling the impression that only well-to-do nuclear families can keep their kids at home. Heather's experience illustrates the possibilites available to a single parent, and underlines the feeling, common to many parents, that it takes many, many people to raise a child.

I AM THE SINGLE PARENT TO ONE DAUGHTER. ALTHOUGH THERE ARE only two of us in our immediate family, our circle stretches far beyond that. When my daughter was still very young I chose to homeschool her. Homeschooling comes with many challenges at the best of times; as a single parent it has some extras. To me the joys of learning with my daughter are worth the sacrifices, and far outweigh the challenges. When I say I am single I am referring to my marital status only. I do not believe that we are meant to do this most important of all jobs, solo—and so I don't. We live a life full of meaning and people.

Megan arrived during a time in my life when I was learning for the pure joy of learning. She was conceived while I was traveling and exploring in Europe with her father. It was a time of awakenings and new beginnings. During my pregnancy I knew that it was important to me that I raise this child in a responsible and thoughtful way. I wanted her to have a strong sense of herself and what she wants out of life. I did not want strangers raising her, and immediately started thinking about ways that I could be at home with her full time. I knew that I did not want someone else caring for my child in a daycare and that I wanted more than the public schools were offering. Five months pregnant and on my own, I came back to Canada to await her birth.

With the birth of my daughter, I became completely and totally immersed in parenting. I read everything I could get my hands on. I devoured alternative parenting magazines and then started reading about education. I was fairly isolated at the time and looking back, I realize that I didn't have many influences—positive or negative—to pressure or sway me, and so had no doubts about following my non-mainstream instincts to have Megan sleep with me, to breastfeed her until she was three years of age, or to raise her as a vegetarian. From her infancy I enjoyed observing and participating in her explorations of the world around her, noting her innate curiosity and unstoppable desire for learning. With more reading, it became so clear to me that homeschooling was the choice that would allow her to remain in this beautiful state of exploration and learning. This decision brought many challenges to my life. At the time I was so determined to do it, I didn't think through how tough things could and would be.

The questions that I am most often asked as a single parent are: "How can you afford it?" "How do you find time for yourself?" and "How do you avoid burnout?" These are all part of one issue—support. Support is a key component of all homeschooling and in fact, a key component of all real education. Creating that support presents many choices and challenges, especially for the single parent.

The greatest challenge for many parents who choose to keep their children home from school seems to be financial. In Megan's early years, one way I found to manage my budget was to share accommodations, childcare, and household chores. Initially I lived with my parents in an extended family situation (an option which may not be available to everyone) and at two separate times, with other single mothers (each had one daughter as well). Besides sharing the rent, the cost of groceries, and the childcare, we shared the cooking, each doing three nights a week—an economic way to give each of us more time to spend with our respective children. This way of living eased our workload substantially and provided myself and the other mom with the support and companionship of another adult when our daughters were young babies and toddlers. It was a wonderful way to create a stable family environment for all, and both Megan and I have very special memories of those times.

In terms of making an income, there are a number of choices for those choosing to homeschool as a single parent. These include going on social assistance, working part-time and arranging childcare, working at home, or working outside of the home in a situation that allows the child to come along. I have experienced each of these. Each, of course, has had its drawbacks as well as its advantages.

On social assistance, I was able to focus all my attention and energy on getting used to being a new mother and getting to know my infant. The down side was the minimum amount of money coming in and the negative feelings associated with receiving welfare.

Working part-time gave me a chance to get out into the world beyond motherhood. I continued to do the work that I had done off and on for years—working as customer service representative in a bank. It was not my favorite job but it paid the bills. Mornings were tough when I would wake my sleeping daughter to dress and feed her, then leave her crying and screaming with a baby-sitter.

Running my own business and working at home provided me with a real sense of responsibility. Shortly after Megan's birth I became involved with childbirth education and support. I taught prenatal classes in the evening, did labor support for couples, and taught the ancient art of infant massage in my home. The challenge was living with the uncertainty regarding the amount of income each month.

Now I work part-time as a consultant with an independent school where I have the flexibility of working from home or going into an office where Megan comes along. I have the wonderful privilege of working with other homelearning families that have registered their children as homeschoolers. We offer a variety of services—a bimonthly newsletter, a computer Bulletin Board System, workshops, and an annual conference for families. In addition to the opportunity to do challenging and fulfilling work, the assurance of regular pay and the advantage of flexibility are huge benefits. The challenge comes when Megan really wants and needs to stay home when I really need to go into the office.

Finding and creating time for one's self is another of the

greatest challenges of being alone at home full time with children. We all know how the best of us can, over time, become overworked, overtaxed, and oversocialized. As many parents have experienced, there are times when one does not even get to go to the toilet alone! Wouldn't it be easier for me to use the free baby-sitting service the public schools have provided for me? At times I think it really would be, believe me! And that is why I believe in finding time to be alone.

For my daughter and I to maintain a healthy relationship, it has been essential to our survival that we help each other out and that we both get times to ourselves every day. I have created this in a number of ways, the primary one being our daily routine. For years Megan has awakened at least an hour before me. She has established her own morning rituals in which she gets breakfast for herself and her three pets, gets dressed, writes in her journal, brushes and braids her hair, and listens to story tapes. (Her passion for a number of years has been audiotapes of books, even more so in the last few months. Some parents teasingly refer to their child as a "bookworm." Poor Meggie gets referred to as a "tapeworm.") In the evening we have a special bedtime routine: Meg goes to bed early while I stay up late. I do my studying and playing then. I often have a friend over for a visit, do my writing, or watch a video, or, if I really need some extra special time, I treat myself to a massage from the massage therapist who lives in the top suite of the house we live in.

Megan has grandparents and an uncle who have been very supportive and involved in her life from the minute she was born. They have always taken their roles with the same seriousness and care that I have as her mother. We are very fortunate that they include her in their lives as a special person. She has regular overnight visits and outings with them.

I love the African proverb, "It takes a whole village to raise a child." For single parents, there is more motivation to find that village. Over the years I have created a wonderful community for Megan and myself. Megan has many people who "parent" and influence her in positive and meaningful ways. Our lives are full of people who go to school, people who don't, straight and gay neighbors and friends, elderly people and babies. I get involved with many community events—I volunteer and manage events and I bring Megan along with me. Often people do not quite understand why my child is with me. Given time, they see that she is a capable and willing worker and an interesting person to talk with as well. Because of this, she has had many opportunities that otherwise may not have presented themselves to her.

In addition, I have always made a conscious effort to know and befriend my neighbors. I make myself available to do childcare, to cook meals and even to walk their children to school. As a result Megan is invited and encouraged to be involved in others' lives. She is easy to have around and people comment on her willingness to help out. I have learned to swallow my independent pride and accept help when I need it. As a result, I am able more easily to take breaks—to take time for myself when it is really needed.

Sometimes things don't go all that smoothly: often I feel that I am doing the job of more than one person; at times I feel lonely and discouraged. But when Megan and I go for walks and I hold her hand in mine, everything feels at it should be. I am incredibly grateful for my family and friends who have always been available and loving to both of us; I know that things would look much different without their support and companionship. I am very content with the life I have created for my daughter and myself. I value the special times we have had together and look forward to many more.

16

Learning as a Lifestyle

Heidi Priesnitz

Growing up in the daily company of one's own family and sharing in the everyday responsibilities of a home-based business goes a long way toward building self-confidence, as Heidi Priesnitz explains in the following article. A reflection of the slogan "Children are people too," Heidi's deschooled childhood has given her the ability to establish her own business as well as to write two books about deschooling: 48 Good Reasons Not to Go to School *and* A Practical Guide to Unschooling for Teenagers, *both published by the Alternate Press.*

MY EXPERIENCE WITH DESCHOOLING HAS BEEN ENTIRELY unstructured. No kitchen table classroom. No parent as teacher. No curriculum. No grades. Nothing remotely school-like at all.

I grew up free of the structure of school, choosing my own paths of study, my own schedule, and my own instructors (if I chose any at all!). Today, as a young adult, I am self-educated, self confident and happily (and successfully) self-employed—partly, I think, because I didn't go to school and partly because I grew up in the family business.

My life without school

I was a very free-spirited little girl. Although I understand that in many situations (such as school), children who are free-spirited are said to be problematic, disruptive, unruly and a whole host of other terrible things, I was encouraged by my family to do my own thing.

Choice was a big factor in my deschooling experience. My

parents helped to guide me through my learning, but ultimately left the choices—and the responsibilities that go with having choices—up to me. I was able to choose what I wanted to learn and when. For that reason learning happened naturally, when I became interested. At one point in my life I chose *not* to attend school, and at another point I chose *to* attend school. I was happy with both realities (in different ways) because they were my choices. To some extent, the experiences complemented each other. And going to school certainly made me appreciate what a wonderful life I had before I went to school.

Near the end of my high school experience, I wrote: "Although at the beginning I was distressed because I thought my home education was getting in the way of my success at school, I soon learned that I actually had many advantages over my peers. Because I was used to a resource-based style of learning, research and independent thinking came far more easily to me than to others. Also my interest and motivation far exceeded that of my peers. It amazed me, and often frustrated me, that everyone else spent their time and energy trying to avoid things, when I was eagerly awaiting them."

Before I went to school, I learned through living. Nothing can prepare you for life nearly as well as *living it*. My parents recognized that the best learning is learning-by-doing, and they facilitated a lot of interesting experiences for me, whether it was driving me across town, paying for courses and lessons, or just including me in their lives.

When I was 14, I wrote: "The place where I think that my deschooling has really paid off is in my attitude and my outlook on life. I feel that because of deschooling, I have a lot more confidence in myself, and in others as well. I also feel that I have a better relationship with my family than I would have otherwise, just because I've been with them a lot more."

I remember as a kid enjoying the slogan "kids are people too," and in my family we were. We were important—our ideas, our needs and our concerns were listened to and taken seriously. We were included in the very real decisions that families (usually adults) must make. We were treated like full-sized people, even though we were small.

Helping with the family business

When I was young my parents made a big lifestyle choice: to start a small business—*Natural Life* magazine. At the beginning, my father pretty much ran the business alone. But soon we all started to get involved. One of the great advantages of small family-run businesses, especially those run out of the home, is that the whole family can quite easily (and sometimes unavoidably) become involved. With Wendy as editor, Rolf soon had more time to pursue the publishing end of things, and as my sister and I got older we took on regular jobs too.

Because neither of us went to school, we had lots of time to take trips with our parents to the printers, or to the bank and post office, or to trade shows. Even when we weren't directly helping, we were learning and observing. Family-run businesses are a natural choice for deschooling families, because parents can work and be with their kids at the same time—and because businesses themselves are great learning experiences.

I was quite unaware until recently that I was an unusual five year old, because I was able to sort mailing labels in postal code order! It was a very natural way for me to help. Sometimes helping was self-motivated: *I want them to play with me, so I'd better help them get these envelopes stuffed.* Or, I'd want to have a bath but there were piles of magazines in the tub that needed to be bundled! Other times I helped because I thought of the business as a family responsibility—not just something that my parents looked after.

This type of direct involvement in money-making activities gave me a real understanding of where money comes from. I knew that if a lot of subscription cheques didn't come in the mail for a few weeks that I wouldn't be able to get new shoes. The other side of that awareness is that I also knew that if I helped, the business would grow stronger. I enjoyed working when I was a kid. We were never forced to help, but always encouraged to if we seemed interested. If Melanie or I took on the responsibility of a certain job, we were always accountable for it. We knew we had to do a good job and were happy to.

Once, when I had been helping with packaging and mailing out book orders, a lady wrote about how pleased she was to receive her order so quickly and in such good condition. As this compliment was passed on to me I remember my mom saying, "I wonder if she knows her books were sent out by a 9 year old?!"

The point is, it didn't matter. The job got done.

Helping with a business in a real way is very rewarding for kids. I felt very important and needed—two things that most people spend a lot of time looking for, even as adults. And with the confidence, experience and knowledge that I gained from helping, I was able to run the business on my own several years ago while my parents were away.

From being involved in a real and practical way from an early age I now have hands-on experience not only in the publishing industry, but in the small business world in general. And now, at the age of 23, when most people my age are struggling to get through college, to find jobs or to figure out what to do with their lives, I've already started a business that I love and am supporting myself with it (with a little help from the old family business!). Because I was deschooled and because I had the chance to do real work on a real business as I was growing up, I already know what I want to do with my life *and* I'm already doing it!

17

Deschooling and Parent Involvement in Education: AllPIE — A Learning Network

Seth Rockmuller and Katharine Houk

This short piece outlines what a learning network can be. When most people imagine a deschooled society, learning networks of various kinds tend to play a prominent role in replacing the social and intellectual connections people often value in schools. The Alliance for Parental Involvement in Education (AllPIE) is one of the best and most ambitious networks, involving all kinds of homeschoolers, deschoolers, and alternative schoolers. Their example is important in envisioning a world beyond schools.

IF WE WANT TO LOOK AT EDUCATION WITH AN EYE TOWARD meaningful change, we all need to deschool ourselves. This is true whether we choose to educate our own children in public school, in private school, or at home. In order to free ourselves from the myths upon which our current educational institutions are based and from the propaganda commonly used to sell schools to the populace, we need to understand the premises upon which the existing system of education is based and to reconsider our own educational experiences against that background. Only then can we begin to consider our children's needs, the choices regarding the best place for them to receive an education, and ways to advocate for them in school or in the community.

Even those parents who have chosen to teach their children at home are not free from the pervasive influence of society-wide definitions of acceptable educational practice. Deciding to homeschool is often the first step on a journey into the meaning of learning. The irony is that, while it often seems to be a critical decision with regard to educational approach, it may simply be the first small step toward much more significant changes in perception. Depending on an individual's personal predilections, those changes may be in the perceived roles of families and governments in raising children, in the part to be played in education by the community, in the consideration of different approaches to learning for reaching different children, in the importance of personal autonomy in education and in life in general, and in a host of other areas.

How do we go about deschooling ourselves? The educational establishment has had enormous influence on the lives of most of us for thirteen or more years. In that time many subtle lessons about education and learning are instilled in each of us. How can we release ourselves from those lessons—emotionally and psychologically, as well as intellectually?

The Alliance for Parental Involvement in Education (AllPIE) helps people to address this question. Originally AllPIE's purpose was to provide information about the wide variety of educational options available to families (public education, private education, and home education), to help people choose the best educational options for their families, and to help parents advocate for their children within the options they choose. It quickly became evident, however, that the core questions always came back to the need for parents and teachers to disentangle themselves from the assumptions of conventional approaches to schooling. Were schools organized to address the ways in which people actually learned, or was educational pedagogy formulated to address the ways in which schools were structured? If the latter is true, what does it mean for children who are learning outside of school or for groups trying to create alternative educational environments, either within or outside the public system?

AllPIE is a forum for gathering information and sharing ideas about education. It is a place to learn about trends in public school reform, about existing educational alternatives in both the public and private sectors, about home education, and about the many ways in which families are reinventing education to meet the needs of their communities. It is a place to gather resources, to learn about learning, and to express opinions and raise questions in a nonjudgmental setting. There is no single "right" way to educate children, and AllPIE's most basic assumption is that parents are the ones best qualified to make decisions about the education of their children.

What does AllPIE's forum look like? Its shape is defined by the publication of two newsletters, *Options in Learning* (national) and the *New York State Home Education News*; by an annual family conference in which adults and children share in learning and building a sense of community; by providing a resources catalogue containing books, audiotapes, back issues of the newsletter, and pamphlets, as well as a mail-order lending library of books about education and parenting; by organizing workshops and retreats at which families can get together to share their successes and concerns; and by establishing AllPIE partner groups where people can join at a local level to build schools, learning centers, home education support groups, and discussion groups. Through the Alliance, parents and teachers can find others who have faced similar problems or dreamed similar dreams.

The Alliance for Parental Involvement in Education provides information about home education, but it is not a homeschooling organization. It provides information about Waldorf, Montessori, and other alternative approaches to education, but it is not a private school organization. It provides information about reforms and other trends in public education, but it is not a public school organization. The Alliance is a family organization which emphasizes the importance of original thought about learning with no artificial boundaries separating learning from other aspects of our lives. As the needs of parents and families grow and change, AllPIE changes with them.

Once families have access to sufficient information and have confidence in their own knowledge and abilities, education becomes a grassroots function, growing from the needs of the community, rather than being handed down by educational experts experimenting on a global level with a succession of unproved theories. It becomes real and meaningful, rather than abstract and easily assessable. It becomes individual and usable, rather than generic and forgettable. It becomes the foundation for a satisfying and responsible life for adults and children alike.

Val Franklin

Part Four — Schools That Ain't: Places That Work

18

Summerhill School

Zoe Readhead

Zoe Readhead is the daugher of A. S. Neill. She was born and educated at Summerhill, the best-known free school in the world, located in England. In 1971 she married Tony Readhead, a local farmer. They have four children, and three of them are currently being educated at Summerhill. Zoe worked for some time at the Lewis Wadham Free School in New York State. A qualified riding teacher, she managed and ran a riding stables near Summerhill, and took over the headship of the school in 1985.

A. S. Neill and Summerhill are what most people think of when they consider alternative education. Zoe has seen Summerhill develop from all kinds of perspectives, as a baby, as a student, as a graduate, and as the head of the school. She is uniquely qualified to comment on A. S. Neill, the history of Summerhill, and the state of the school today.

A. S. NEILL WAS BORN IN FORFAR, SCOTLAND, IN 1883, THE FOURTH of thirteen children of the village schoolmaster or "Dominie," a stern, puritanical man who ruled his classroom with a rod of iron. In those days the strap or "tawse" was commonly used in schools in Scotland and when at the age of 15 Neill was taken on as a pupil-teacher by his father, he was expected to use it on the other children. His father cared little for him and made it clear that he thought him both dull and unworthy.

At the age of 25 Neill went to Edinburgh University and took a degree in English. Afterwards he became a journalist and then Head of a small school in Gretna Green. It was there that he wrote his first book, *A Dominie's Log*, and began to form his ideas on freedom for children. After a year in the school he wrote:

I have converted a hard-working school into a playground, and I rejoice. These bairns have had a year of happiness and liberty. They have done what they liked; they have sung their songs while they were working at graphs, they have eaten their sweets while they read their books, they have hung on my arms as we rambled along in search of artistic corners.

In 1913 Neill visited Homer Lane's Little Commonwealth, a community for delinquent adolescents, and saw self-government at work. A firm believer in the innate goodness of children, Lane acquainted Neill with Freud's *New Psychology* and later became his psychoanalyst. Thus he introduced Neill to two elements that were essential to the founding of Summerhill: the self-government meeting and the importance of a child's emotional well-being over academic development.

Summerhill was founded in 1921 in Germany, in Hellerau, a suburb of Dresden, as part of an international school, The Neue Schule. There were wonderful facilities there and a lot of enthusiasm but over the following months Neill became progressively less happy with the school. He felt it was run by idealists—they disapproved of tobacco, foxtrots and cinemas— while he wanted the children to live their own lives. He said:

> I am only just realizing the absolute freedom of my scheme of Education. I see that all outside compulsion is wrong, that inner compulsion is the only value. And if Mary or David wants to laze about, lazing about is the one thing necessary for their personalities at the moment. Every moment of a healthy child's life is a working moment. A child has no time to sit down and laze. Lazing is abnormal, it is a recovery, and therefore it is necessary when it exists.

Together with Frau Neustatter (later to be his first wife), Neill moved his school to Austria. The setting, on top of a mountain, was idyllic, but the local people—a Catholic community—were hostile. By 1923 Neill had moved to a town in the South of England, Lyme Regis, and a house called Summerhill where he settled down until 1927 when he moved to the present site at Leiston in the county of Suffolk. Neill continued to run the school with his second wife, Ena, until he died in 1973. She then took over until her retirement in 1985 when their daughter, Zoe, and her husband took over.

Summerhill today has not changed fundamentally since it was first started. Its aims could be described as the following:

To allow children freedom to grow emotionally;

To give children power over their own lives;

To give children the time to develop naturally;

To create a happier childhood by removing fear and coercion by adults.

Allowing children freedom helps to develop self-motivation. Emotionally healthy individuals are not inhibited in their learning process. Giving children power over their own lives promotes a feeling of self-worth and of responsibility to others. They learn from an early age that what they think is important and that others will listen to what they have to say.

Giving children time to develop means letting them play and play and play for as long as they want to. Only through free, imaginative play can a child develop the skills needed for adulthood. Just as a kitten learns to hunt by chasing leaves and insects, so a child prepares for adult life by playing with other children. Within the group all the qualities, good and bad, that will be encountered later, are present. By making mistakes the child grows and matures without the need for morals to be taught. Neill constantly stressed the innate goodness of children and urged us to have patience and trust that they would learn these things for themselves.

Summerhill is a community of approximately 80 people, adults and children. There are usually 12 staff and an international group of children. At the present time about a third are from Japan while the rest are divided between English and European. Summerhill is less well known in its own country than anywhere else.

It is a self-governing community—which means that all the decisions regarding daily life are made by the whole group. An important aspect of this is that the business side, the hiring and firing of staff, the intake of pupils, etc., is not the responsibility of the children. They are not asked to take on responsibilities which would be inappropriate or arduous for them. Children have a very real interest in what time they go to bed at night but little in who pays the electricity bills!

The school decision-making process is democratic. Each adult and child has an equal vote. Thus the youngest child has the same voting power as a staff member. Not only do the children have equal power in school meetings, they also vastly outnumber the adults. Most teachers' reaction to this is one of fear—imagine what would happen in a conventional school if all the pupils outnumbered the staff in a vote! Total anarchy? Loss of all moral codes? Possibly—but in Summerhill, because of the freedom they have experienced, most of the pupils are already socially responsible and are used to thinking about the needs of the group rather than their own. This does not mean that there are never disputes or disagreements; one of the important lessons learned has been that the needs of children and adults are very different indeed!

The following is an example of a typical School Meeting. The older kids in the school wanted to have no bedtime and proposed that they could stay up as late as they liked provided that they stick to the silence hour which is 10:30 p.m. There was a long discussion about it as many people had things to say on the subject. Some were worried about the possible noise, others about lack of sleep. Eventually the vote was taken and the motion was carried that they try it for one week to see if it could work. A week or so later there was a special meeting because one of the staff had been woken up several times with noise in the night. The community decided that the older kids had had their chance and should get their bedtimes back again.

Occasionally there are rebellious children who want to break all the school laws and go against the community in whatever way they can. Sometimes such a child can whip up enough support to get some school laws dropped or changed. Obviously it can be a bit disruptive but it is a good learning experience and in most cases is quickly put right. What better way to learn to be a law-abiding citizen than to try living without laws?

Summerhill believes in freedom but not licence. This means that you are free to do as you like—but you must not interfere with somebody else's freedom. You are free to go to lessons or stay away because that is your own personal business and you can make the choice. But you cannot play your drum kit at four in the morning because that would interfere with the freedom of others. Within this structure there are probably more laws in Summerhill than any other school in the country—about 190 at the last count! They range from what time you have to be in bed at night to where you are allowed to shoot bows and arrows. Here is a random selection of them:

Only twelve-year-olds and over are allowed sheath knives.

You must have a working front and back brake on your bike.
You can't ride little kids' bikes—even with permission.
You can't watch TV during lessons or meal times.
Writing graffiti—£1.00 fine (but there is a special wall where you are allowed to).
Breaking bedtime laws—half hour community work.

There are School Meetings twice a week, one on Friday afternoon and one on Saturday evening. The Friday meeting is called Tribunal and is used for people to bring cases against one another. Thus, if somebody has been riding your bike without permission or has broken into your box to nick your cash, you can bring it up in the tribunal.

Chairing the meeting is a difficult task. Although nobody is exactly unruly, it is demanding to keep up to 70 people of different ages sitting quietly for about an hour at a time. The Chairperson has ULTIMATE power! You can be fined for making noise, moved, or thrown out altogether. It is a strangely formal occasion and visitors have often remarked how much more ordered it is than the House of Commons!

Sometimes teachers bring up children for being unruly in class. One such case recently carried the fine that the culprit should be banned from lessons for three days—but the child appealed it on the grounds that it was too severe! Naturally the staff can be brought up, too. It is a very leveling experience to be brought up before the whole community—especially if you have been teaching in the conventional system. Some new staff find it too much and are very embarrassed about it. But it is a valuable experience for grown-ups to be put in a position where they *can* be brought up by children and fined accordingly. Possibly the whole educational system would benefit if all teachers were put into that situation, if only for the experience of it. The face of teaching would change if all teachers had a class that could get up and walk out if they were not interested, as they do at Summerhill. Teaching to a captive audience is one thing; having to hold people's interest is quite another!

Summerhill is now an old and respected institution among progressive-minded educationalists. It continually struggles both financially and with the Department of Education but so far, it is keeping its head above water! A proud place with many friends throughout the world, Summerhill is eager to make new connections and very willing to share any helpful experiences.

19

A History of the Albany
Free School and Community

Chris Mercogliano

Chris Mercogliano has been a teacher at the Free School in Albany, New York, since 1973, working with children from ages two to fourteen. In 1987 he was named co-director. An environmental activist, he has recently been appointed to the mayor's advisory committee on recycling and waste reduction. He is also an essayist, poet, organic farmer, mason, plumber, and journeyman carpenter, and is currently writing a book about his experiences at the Free School over the past twenty years.

The Albany Free School, a truly amazing place, has been operating for more than twenty-five years, largely centering around its founder, Mary Leue. The school has expanded into a genuine community, including a natural foods store, a family life clinic, an investment group, a number of houses, and a wilderness retreat. The scope of the project is inspiring, and demonstrates how a genuine community-based experience can be created within a city.

FOUNDED IN 1969 BY MARY LEUE, THE FREE SCHOOL IN ALBANY, NEW York, is one of the oldest inner-city independent alternative schools in the country. Operating on a sliding tuition scale that slides all the way to zero when necessary, we are a learning community of about forty-five children, with many from low-income families, and eight full-time teachers supported by numerous talented and creative volunteers and interns. We have thrived by developing an internal economy which enables us to avoid dependence on outside grants from government or the private sector, or on prohibitively high tuitions. (Never in our history have we turned a single child away for financial reasons.)

Over the years a group of about 35 (at last count)—Free School teachers, parents, children and others interested in exploring the realities of living and working together in community—has coalesced around the school and has gradually developed a more consciously spiritual dimension which has nourished deeper and more permanent community roots. Our still-evolving "spiritual tradition" is multifaceted, drawing from many diverse paths as we continue to seek out ways to draw ourselves closer to God and to each other. Our guiding principle could best be called what has been known through the ages as the Perennial Philosophy whose tenets lie at the core of all forms of religious practice.

According to Aldous Huxley, in his introduction to a 1944 translation of the *Bhagavad-Gita*, the Perennial Philosophy consists of four central doctrines:

1. The material world is a manifestation of the Divine Ground from which it derives its being;

2. Human beings are capable of a direct experience of that Divine Ground, in such a way that the knower unites with the known;

3. Human Beings have a double nature, a temporal ego and an eternal self, which is the divine spark within each of us, and which we can identify with at any time;

4. Human life on earth has but one true purpose: to identify with our eternal selves and seek out a unitive understanding of the Divine Ground.

As I will attempt to portray in this brief sketch, The Free School has acted like the dust particle at the center of every rain drop—or the irritating grain of sand which inspires the growth of the pearl! The story of how this meandering, organic development has occurred will best explain the what and the why of our school and community. At no point has there been a five-year plan or a single guiding philosophy or model; rather at every step, function and necessity—with occasional outside inspiration—have dictated form and process, and there has always been a fascinating parallel between the internal growth of each participating individual and the external growth of the school and the community.

Put more simply, from day one we've been making it up as we go along. Lacking money, we've had to become our own experts, hashing out our own solutions together, and learning from our numerous mistakes along the way. As Rabbi Zalman Schachter-

Shalomi, a wonderfully sage leader of the Jewish Renewal Movement, once said to us in one of our workshops, "The only way to get it together is together!" The eternal challenge seems to be trying to live out, on a daily basis, the basic principles of love, truthfulness, emotional honesty, peer-level leadership, and cooperation which are at the heart of the Free School's philosophy of education. (Reb Zalman calls this "Walking your talk.")

The term "community" is grossly over- and ill-used these days and therefore, I think, it's important first to define it carefully. As far as I'm concerned, M. Scott Peck has written *the* book on community, and I always like to refer back to one of his definitions in *The Different Drum* :

> If we are going to use the word meaningfully we must restrict it to a group of individuals who have learned how to communicate honestly with each other, whose relationships go deeper than their masks of composure, and who have developed some significant commitment to rejoice together, mourn together and to delight in each other, making others' condition our own.

The Free School was born, of necessity, when Mary returned to Albany with her husband, Bill, and their five children, from Oxford where Bill had been studying while on sabbatical from the State University of New York where he was a professor of philosophy. Mary's youngest son, Mark, was miserable in his fifth grade class at one of the "better" Albany Public Schools. Mary made every attempt to address the problem with both the teacher and principal, and with no change in sight, Mark began refusing to go at all, asking if, instead, his mother would teach him at home. At this moment, the Free School's basic operating strategy was born: Do it first, ask permission later. When Mary received a threatening call from the principal, she sprang into action to establish the legality of teaching her son at home. She managed to find a man in the curriculum department of the State Education Department who told her that her decision was legal and who offered to give "state guidelines" to any school official who hassled her. Sure enough, the school district's truant officer called Mary the next day and began issuing all sorts of final warnings. Mary calmly gave him the name of the official in State Education and then, not long after, the truant officer, who is actually the head of the district's Bureau of Attendance and Guidance, called again to apologize and to offer assistance. Ironically, this man, Joe

Markham, would later become our official liaison with the superintendent of schools and a trusted and powerful ally! Thus Mark Leue became perhaps New York State's first legal homeschooler.

But not for long. Two weeks later, Mary ran into a friend who had three children who were suffering in another of Albany's finest schools and she immediately begged Mary to take them on. Mary agreed on the spot, not wanting her son to be isolated alone with her at home, and, presto! a school was born. At that point, Mary decided to visit other "free schools" such as Jonathan Kozol's Roxbury Community School in Cambridge, Massachusetts, and Orson Bean's Fifteenth Street School in New York City, and then to hold alternative education forums around town. Suddenly four students became seven, two teachers climbed aboard, and the need for a building was obvious.

For both pragmatic and socio-political reasons, Mary decided to locate the new school in the inner-city. First of all, property in the ghetto was cheap; and secondly, Mary wanted a fully integrated school, with the onus placed on white, middle-class families to bring their children out of their uptown enclaves. So, an old church building was rented temporarily until Mary found and purchased an abandoned parochial school building in the same South End neighborhood.

Two important developments occurred in the early tumultuous years of rapid growth, with parents struggling over educational philosophy and practice and with kids from opposite ends of the socio-economic spectrum thrashing out their own issues. A firm policy was established that only those actually present day-to-day in the building could determine the school's operating policy. Others were welcome to attend meetings and to advise and suggest, but that would be the extent of their power. This absolute internal autonomy remains a cornerstone of our methodology, such as it is. Next, in order to empower the kids to hold up their end of the bargain, and to give them a way to work out their differences (which were many in that initial period) nonviolently, Mary and the other teachers instituted a "council meeting" system, whereby anyone with a serious problem could call a meeting at any time, with everyone dropping what they were doing to attend. Meetings were run by Roberts' Rules and therefore anyone, with sufficient support, could set policy, make or change rules, etc. The council meeting structure provided a measure of safety for all, and ensured that, borrowing A. S. Neill's phrase, freedom didn't become licence. Later, the "stop rule" was borrowed from Jerry Mintz's Shaker Mountain School in Vermont. The rule is quite simple: if you want someone to stop doing something to you, you just tell them firmly to stop and if they don't, you then call a council meeting to get support in dealing with the aggressor.

One of the valuable lessons Mary learned from Jonathan Kozol was the importance of freeing the school from becoming tuition-dependent (and therefore essentially middle-class), by developing some sort of business. Mary had the vision, bolstered with a small inheritance from her mother, to buy and fix up some of the abandoned buildings on the same block as the school building. We have rehabilitated ten of them so far, for use as teacher housing and for generating income in various ways.

Teaching at the young school was an intense experience, with all of us who were working there full-time truly living on the edge. Salaries, when we got paid at all, were minuscule, and many of the kids we were working with were in crisis most of the time. A number of us were attempting to live together semi-communally in school-owned housing, and so the interpersonal dimension of the whole enterprise was pretty frothy, to say the least. It gradually became apparent that a forum was needed in which the adults could resolve conflicts and deepen their communication with and understanding of each other. Mary suggested we start a weekly "group" where we could both clear up unfinished interpersonal issues, and safely delve into areas of intrapersonal emotional (and later spiritual) growth. Our four-to-five-hour Wednesday evening group has now been meeting continuously since 1974 and is another absolute cornerstone of both school and community, and unquestionably is the key to the longevity of both.

Over the next few years, some of the teachers as well as Free School parents began buying dilapidated houses on the block for themselves and then applying the rehabilitation skills that we had learned while repairing the school buildings toward the creation of our own homes. A number of us were able to qualify for low-income, "sweat equity" Housing and Urban Development grants, which largely solved the financial aspect of this important step. We helped each other on our houses a great deal during this time, and a budding sense of real community began to grow, fed by the shared labor, risk, and excitement.

This expanding group energy, combined with a growing set of

practical needs, led to the establishment of several "community institutions." As a number of us began to have children of our own, Mary, with assistance from my wife Betsy, also a teacher in the school who dreamed of becoming a midwife (and now is a fine one), started the Family Life Center. The Center provides pregnancy and childbirth support of all kinds and teaches a variety of forms of medical self-care for both adults and children.

With home-ownership and growing families came the need to manage carefully what little money we had and the need for loans at affordable rates: hence what Mary named "The Money Game," which is part credit union and part cooperative investment group, for those of us who would otherwise be shut out from such mysterious rites of post-industrial capitalism. Then Mary and another Free School teacher, Nancy, each of whom had started a natural foods store in their past lives, collaborated on one for the community; we now have twenty-four-hour a day access to whole foods at low cost. A small book store and crafts co-op were later added on, managed by yet another teacher, Connie.

Finally, we all began yearning for a place away from the city where we could vacation together and where we could retreat as needed. Larry, a Free School parent and community member and a master bargain hunter, found a "camp" on a small lake about twenty-five miles outside of Albany. With two forty-foot living rooms, six large bedrooms and two kitchens, it was just what we were looking for; furthermore, the owner was looking to sell quickly because it was beginning to need substantial repairs. We practically bought it on the spot! Rainbow Camp, as we christened it, is now a multi-purpose facility, used by the community for retreats and vacations, by the school for day- and week-long trips with the kids, and by Rainbow Camp Association for its weekend workshop programs focusing on personal, relational, and spiritual growth, and on ecology and earth survival. Any profit from the workshops goes toward paying for camp upkeep and taxes.

To make one final long story short, the purchase of Rainbow Camp led to us meeting an older man, Hank Hazelton, who dreamed of turning his 250 acres of woods, located just over the hill from our new camp, into a wilderness living center and sanctuary. After several crippling strokes, Hank decided to give his land to the Free School so that we would carry out his vision for him. Currently, we are in the process of building an octagonal "teaching lodge," twenty-four feet in diameter, in the heart of the forest, and are working with the Audubon Society of New York State to open a cooperative wildlife sanctuary on the land. A significant piece of the future of both the Free School and the community seems to lie in this direction, though, as before, there is little in the way of a long range plan. We will continue to trust in God (but tie our camels!), and let one step lead us to the next.

20

A School for Today

Mimsy Sadofsky

Ms. Sadofsky was one of the group that founded Sudbury Valley School in 1968, and has been deeply involved in the establishment of over a dozen other schools throughout the world based on a similar educational philosophy. She has served in a wide variety of capacities at the school, has spoken extensively in public forums about education, has written several articles, and is co-author of the books, Legacy of Trust *and* Kingdom of Childhood, *published by Sudbury Valley School Press. She has three children, all of whom attended SVS for virtually their entire schooling.*

LIKE THE ALBANY FREE SCHOOL, SUDBURY VALLEY SCHOOL (SVS) has been around for more than a quarter-century, with an amazing community and incredible facilities, and is equally successful. SVS, however, has thrived outside the city, largely self-contained. The school is particularly important in that it has been the model for literally dozens of other free schools around the world, and its philosophy is widely disseminated.

In 1968, the group of people who started Sudbury Valley School in Framingham, Massachusetts, began by examining the values common in American society in order to determine what values should guide our schools.

How, we asked, can a school best foster creativity? The answer was amazingly simple—and amazingly complex. People are learners. They are born already working on their education! They are born curious—and striving. How else can you explain the unbelievable development in the first few years of life from a pretty much helpless infant, with only the most fundamental communication skill, into a walking, talking toddler whose universe expands exponentially from month to month. They are born creative. No one at all has to explain learning processes to an infant. You can't stop them, and each one learns differently: how to roll over, or to sit up, how to explore with their fingers, to stand, to walk, to say a few words and then a few sentences, and then express an infinite number of thoughts, many complex and abstract. Infants begin life learning in the ways we all use when we are learning for our own pleasure. They explore. They imitate. They experience. They build more complex world views from trial and error. It is simple to understand, but terribly difficult to accept, that the individual is best served at every age by allowing that native curiosity and creativity to be undeflected and un-interrupted; that the best schooling may be the schooling that least impedes the mind's free exploration of the environment.

Why don't we have schools today that allow a tremendous amount of individual freedom to follow curiosity? Why do we have schools today that have not incorporated the basic notion that an individual has, from earliest childhood, a world view, and that each individual hungers constantly to expand that world view, to expand the size of their bubble, to bring what is outside their bubble in, to refine their perception of the world? To learn.

What is the school like? How do these principles get put into practice?

First, let me set the stage. The school enrols students from the age of four up. No one is too old, although most of our students are nineteen or younger. The people in the school, no matter what age they are, are each doing what they want to do. Usually that means that some people are doing things with others, who can be of the most various of ages, and some people are doing things alone. Usually it means that most people are doing things not done in most other schools, and some are doing things that are done in other schools with a very unusual intensity and concentration. It more often means that children are teaching adults than that adults are teaching children, but most often people are learning while unconscious that "learning" is taking place. Doing what they choose to do is the common theme; learning is the by-product. It is first and foremost a place where students are free to follow their inner dictates. They are free to do what we all do when we have the time to, and what we all find to be most satisfactory—they play.

Play is the most serious pursuit at Sudbury Valley. This is not an accident. Psychologists pretty much agree these days that allowing the mind to roam freely has the most potential for mind-expansion. In fact, when we talk about our most creative moments, we describe them as "playing with new ideas." This is a process that cannot be forced. Creativity can grow only in such freedom. Some people play at games, and some play at things which we who have more traditional educations are more comfortable with—writing or art or mathematics or music. But we are quite clear at Sudbury Valley that it is doing what you want to that counts! We have no curriculum and place no value on one pursuit over another. The reason that we are secure in feeling this way is that we constantly see that people play more and more sophisticated "games," explore more and more deeply, that they constantly expand their knowledge of the world, and their ability to handle themselves in it.

Children who play constantly do not draw an artificial line between work and play. In fact, you could say that they are working constantly if you did not see the joy in the place, a joy most usually identified with the pursuit of avocations.

The school has about twenty-five rooms, in two separate buildings. On an average rainy day it is teeming with activity. The rooms are small and large, many are special purpose rooms, like shops and labs, but most are furnished like rather shabby living or dining rooms in homes: lots of sofas, easy chairs, and tables. Lots of people sitting around talking, reading, and playing games. On an average rainy day—quite different from a beautiful, suddenly snowy day, or a warm spring or fall day—most people are inside. But there will also be more than a few who are outside in the rain, and later will come in dripping and trying the patience of the few people inside who think the school should perhaps be a "dry zone." There may be people in the photolab developing or printing pictures they have taken. There may be a karate class, or just some people playing on mats in the dance room. Someone may be building a bookshelf in the woodworking shop in the barn—or fashioning chain mail armor and discussing medieval history. There are almost certainly a few people, either together or separate, making music of one kind or another, and others listening to music of one kind or another. You might find a French class, or Latin, or algebra. You will find adults in groups that include kids, or maybe just talking with one student. It would be most unusual if there were not people playing a computer game somewhere, or chess; a few people doing some of the school's administrative work in the office—while others hang around just enjoying the atmosphere of an office where interesting people are always making things happen; there will be people engaged in role-playing games; other people may be rehearsing a play—it might be original, it might be a classic. They may intend production or momentary amusement. People will be trading stickers and trading lunches. There will probably be people selling things. If you are lucky, someone will be selling cookies they baked at home and brought in to earn money. Sometimes groups of kids have cooked something to sell in order to raise money for an activity—perhaps they need to buy a new kiln, or want to go on a trip. An intense conversation will probably be in progress in the smoking room, and others in other places. A group in the kitchen may be cooking—maybe pizza or apple pie. Always, either in the art room or in any one of many other places, people will be drawing. In the art room they might also be sewing, or painting, and some are quite likely to be working with clay, either on the wheel or by hand. Always there are groups talking, and always there are people quietly reading here and there.

One of the things most adults notice first about Sudbury Valley is the ease of communication. People, no matter what their age, look right at each other, and treat each other with tremendous consideration and easy respect. Fear is absent. There is a comfortable air of self-confidence, the confidence normal to people pursuing the goals they set themselves. Things are almost never quiet, and there is (to an outsider) an exhausting intensity, but the activity is not chaotic or frenetic. Visitors speak of a feeling of a certain order, even though it is clearly a place full of enthusiasm.

The students at Sudbury Valley are "doin' what comes natur'ly." But they are not necessarily choosing what comes easily. A close look discovers that everyone is challenging her or himself; that every kid is acutely aware of her or his own weaknesses and strengths, and is extremely likely to be working hardest on her or his weaknesses. If the weaknesses are social, the child is very unlikely to be stuck away in a quiet room with a book. And if athletics are hard, the child is likely to be outdoors playing basketball. Along with the ebullient good spirits, there is an underlying seriousness—even the six-year-olds know that they, and only they, are responsible for their education. They have been given the gift of tremendous trust, and they understand that this gift is as big a responsibility as it is a delight. They are acutely aware that very young people are not given this much freedom or this much responsibility almost anywhere in the world. But growing up shouldering this responsibility makes for a very early confidence in your own abilities—you get, as one graduate says, a "track record." Self-motivation is never even a question. That's all there is. An ex-student has described some of these effects:

> "There are a lot of things about Sudbury Valley that I think are on a personal level, that build your character, things that perhaps enable you to learn better, that public school students never have a chance to achieve. When you're responsible for your own time, and spend it the way that you want to, you tend to put a lot more enthusiasm into what you do, instead of being a lethargic lump that's molded and prodded into a certain direction. And when you end up the way you want to end up, you know you've been responsible for it. It's a lot more rewarding, I think, than when you end up the way somebody else wants you to end up."

Who are the kids in this school? Are they chosen for creativity, intelligence, or perhaps some other standard? It is a private school—does that mean it appeals to only the well-to-do? Admission is on a first-come, first-served basis, and we have never been full. That means that the students in this school consist of everyone who wants to come whose parents will allow them to. It includes the cerebral and the super-active, the "regular" and the "zeroed-in"—the full gamut of possibilities. Most of the families who choose to send their children to SVS are looking for something they wish they could find in public schools, but cannot: simple freedom for their children to develop according to their own timetables and their own desires. Is it perfection? Hardly. But it is tremendously stimulating and exciting.

Sudbury Valley is a functioning democracy. There is a School Meeting which meets once a week to take care of all the management work, either by directly accomplishing it or by delegating it. Each student and each staff member has one vote, and the meetings are run in an extremely orderly fashion. The School Meeting makes a budget each year, ever so carefully, because the tuition is low and it is important to be thrifty and not to spend money needlessly. Yes, kids know this, and are much harsher judges of what is—or is not—a necessary expense. The School Meeting passes every rule, often after weeks of soul-searching debate. This includes the rule about "no littering," the rules about not ever setting a foot in the pond, the rules that govern which rooms eating is okay in, and which ones you can play the radio in, as well as the rules protecting individual rights. It is up to the School Meeting to approve groups organizing to pursue special interests that want budgets or space. Anyone who thinks that young children are not wise about these matters need only attend a few such school meetings.

The School Meeting delegates some tasks to subgroups or to people elected by them to carry out certain responsibilities. A sub-group called the Public Relations Committee is composed of people interested in the school's public relations work; others serve on the school's Bookkeeping Committee. Someone is elected to see to the Grounds' Maintenance. Another person is elected to keep computer records of all of the judicial activities. All of us are totally accountable and totally aware of our accountability every minute. The School Meeting also debates candidates for staff, votes on them in an all day, school-wide, secret balloting, and awards contracts according to needs determined by this balloting. There is no tenure.

There is also a sub-group of the school meeting set up to deal with rule infractions. It is called the Judicial Committee, and its function is to investigate written complaints about possible rule violations, and to see that justice is served, being constantly careful about due process. Does it work? You bet it does. Peer justice is amazingly effective. Rules are often broken, but the culprits are usually good natured about both admitting what has happened and accepting their punishment.

We have no curriculum. If you send your children to this school, however, there are some certainties about what they learn. They learn how to debate, and how to ask for what they want, and see to it that they get it. They learn to ponder ethical questions. They learn how to concentrate: they can focus on things the way few adults that I know can, and this gives results. The same focus that a five-year-old puts into sand castles, a seven-year-old puts into drawing, an eleven-year-old into making a gingerbread house, a nine-year-old into chess, a twelve-year-old into Dungeons and Dragons, an eight-year-old into climbing forty feet up in the beech tree, a fifteen-year-old into writing a story, a seventeen-year-old into making armor, or an eighteen-year-old into preparing for graduation. That kind of preparation will serve them well in each and every pursuit they choose as adults.

21

A Wonder Story Told by a Young Tree

ilana cameron

ilana cameron is 17 and currently a member of the Virtual High learning community in Vancouver, British Columbia. She loves writing and travelling and playing her didjeridoo. She has self-published a book of her own poetry, and is exploring more and more deeply her inner self and the world around her.

ilana has never been to school, and has a particular easy and contained dignity about her. She writes here about her experiences growing up in a deschooled learning environment, and her perspective helps make the theory and words come to life.

THIS TALE BEGINS WITH A TREE. A TREE TO WONDER UNDER. A TREE TO become one under. A tree to bloom under. A tree that is flexible and always growing and changing, the ilana tree.

ilana was born into a world of three, (mom, dad, and me), and lived happily, beneath trees, with love holding like arms. And arms holding with love.

She was born whole, alive, curious, and trusting.

Soon her life was filled with apples, animals, and trees. She loved so many things in the country. She loved playing in the sand and going to the store. She loved having the special berry-flavored black tea and staring at her favorite ice-cream sandwich in the freezer.

She would write even though she didn't know English letters, she would sing even though she didn't know any songs. She knew only her own, she knew herself.

Soon she became curious about letters and began to read. She read her Heidi book and loved to know that someone else drank goat's milk just like her. Then she lost interest in words and forgot she had known what they meant.

Life carried on in this way. Her life was filled with love and trees.

She went to day care. She loved it there, there were so many things to do and she could do them whenever she wanted. Or she could just sit in the sandbox and practise whistling (and driving the other kids crazy).

She was getting older and her best friend was going to kindergarten. So she went, too. She had to get up at six in the morning and get on the bus. But that was okay because her best friend was there. On the days that her friend wasn't there ilana was terrified. Encountering the kids on the bus and being at school without her friend was scary—an adventure she didn't enjoy.

In kindergarten there were lots of things to do, but you had to do them at certain times. There were times to play with the toys and there were times to play with the games in the boxes, there were times for everything. One day she was swinging on a swing when the bell rang. She realized she didn't want to go inside. Everything was so big and all she was supposed to do was do what other people did.

ilana decided she liked day care much better. So back to day care she went.

The recession hit and soon her parents closed down their natural food store and restaurant; they were now in debt and jobless. So off dad went to the big city, Vancouver, the city full of buildings and cars instead of trees and animals. He started working for a friend. Mom and ilana joined him. Mom became a nurse again and all was new, and strange.

ilana was six years old and her dad told her that most kids her age were going to school. If she wanted they could look around for a good teacher and a school that she would like to go to.

After looking at many schools, ilana said. "Dad, i know who i want as a teacher, i want you. Let's make our home the school, and we'll do what we've always done."

ilana's mom and dad talked with her for several days and then they all agreed to create a school in their home.

My mom got very excited as she was exploring for a name. When she found this quote from Lao Tzu— "From wonder into

wonder/ Existence opens" —the name blossomed in her mind.
Wondertree.

We decided we would continue doing what we had done since i was born. Learning in the world, living in wonder and playing. The name was a coming together of our connection as a family with the symbol of a tree and the wonder we had in our hearts. My name is Hebrew for young tree, flexible and always growing.

Dad created Wondertree. i created Wondertree. Mom created Wondertree.

We put up posters about meetings. No one came. Dad did odd carpentry jobs and mom worked full time as a nurse.

As a family we would discuss how many kids, what we would do, and why we were doing this. Wondertree existed in our hearts as our love, our love for each other and the world. When a man showed up at one of our evening meetings and brought his son to our house, we did what we had always done.

i remember the day he arrived. Jonathan was so timid that he hid behind his dad's legs. i was watching Sesame Street at the time. Jonathan came and watched it with me. He became the second student in Wondertree. So for a while it was just Jonathan and me, watching Sesame Street and wondering in the world. We made houses out of old fridge boxes, and slid down stairs until our bums were numb. We played in the park and asked dad questions as he made things in his workshop. We would make candles with mom, or we'd invent our own games sitting in the back yard.

When more kids came we did what we had always done. We'd drum, and play in the back yard, and talk and bake, and most importantly of all, we would play monster in the park. The thrill of a monster after me, a big scary and yet safe monster chasing me. There was that edge of, oh no, don't catch me! The thrill of running and hiding, and also being the monster. i remember it as one of the most important things we did. We played it almost every week for many years. Sometimes it was gnomes and trolls or IT; they were all variations on the same theme. Chase, run, play, hide, laugh, scream, yelp, and be in utter playing ecstasy. My favorite place to play monster was in the woods. i would hide behind old stumps, and run as fast as i could without getting smacked in the face by tree branches. i would sneak silently through the woods with my pal, secret detective agent Josh.

We were becoming a small community, a family. Every morning we would sit in a circle. We would talk and share with each other.

Any topic could be our discussion. It was so unpredictable: we'd go from talking about someone whose pet had given birth, to a hunger problem in Ethiopia. We would set an hour meeting time and we would go for three. Our minds were alive. We were excited and impassioned about our world.

We learned to notice what we saw in our mind, we learned to write words in there so we could look at them whenever we wanted. We went on magical journeys with our imaginations. We discovered we could stretch ourselves in ways we never knew possible. We did pottery, and drama, continually discovering how we worked.

Who created Wondertree? Every single person who was involved—the parents, mentors, learners, sisters; everyone created it.

We took the wisdom of child and the wisdom of adult and created a union. We were a community based on consensus. Every single person chose to be there and was there because they were supported by the whole community.

We would find mentors and mentors would find us. They were enthusiastic and passionate about something we were interested in. Some of the people we found were: potters, painters, mathematicians, mimes, dancers, yoga masters, writers, and puppeteers.

What does Wondertree smell like? Like clay and bread. Like cuisinare rods and grass. What does it look like? Like sky and cats giving birth. Like couches and a round table. Like friendly faces. What does it sound like? Like birds and laughter. Like dad's voice and singing. What does it feel like? Like toes and sand. Like love and hands.

There were also many tough times. Times when i wondered why i was there, what we were doing, and if i could stand being around my dad every day in such an intense way. Every community that i know of has its jiggles and upsets. We had many and because of our principles we could work most of them out. Sometimes we didn't: some people left Wondertree angrily. There are things i would change the next time round.

Wondertree is only a set of philosophies, and the Wondertree center i was involved in was certainly not perfect. And yet we were there together, saying yes, and seeing what happened. We explored our own minds, ourselves. We learned about ourselves. Our curriculum was ourselves. We were our own textbooks. We learned to understand ourselves. We were a family. We were happy, and we were learning.

Wondertree is based on simple things. The dynamics of being in a group were never simple, though. We all learned and grew as we tried to work as a group. New people would come, old people would go. People were deschooling, people were changing. It took a lot of patience and understanding on everyone's part to function on the basis of consensus. There were misunderstandings, upsets, and arguments.

There were a lot of good times. We did what kids do best, we played and explored. The world was our oyster.

My father understands that it is vital that children follow their own rhythms. We give adults the power to decide what they want to learn; kids have that same right. We are all human, whatever our age. Everyone has the right and responsibility to learn what they want to learn.

One of my biggest lessons is being exactly who i am and being exactly where i am. Being me, here, now. It is so simple and yet so easy to forget. i am here right now. There is only the present, the beautiful, excruciating, limitless, and boundless, present.

i couldn't read very well until around age ten. Then i decided i wanted to be able to read any book i wanted. People around me were reading, people read to me, and i decided that i now wanted to read, too. So i sat down with my dad and started reading to him. He tells me that i asked him not to correct me unless i asked him to. Apparently, i worked most of the words out myself and only needed help for a few of them. For the first month, i read books with lots of pictures. Then i decided that i wanted to read one of my favorite books, *A Wrinkle in Time*. My mom had already read it to me twice that year. My dad thinks the secret was that i had a movie of the book in my head and that i projected the pictures onto the words.

Once i started reading there was no stopping me. My parents soon lost me to the wondrous world of ink and page, the land of imagination. Before i could really read, sometimes my parents tried to get me to read to them. i remember resisting and feeling indignant. i am glad in the end they let me read when i wanted to. Within three years of learning how to read i was reading at a "university level." For example, when i was at the university, where my dad was getting his Masters Degree, i became interested in the description of an English literature course. i went to the

English department with dad and found that the course was taught by the head of the department. It was a course about Victorian and Romantic literature. We went and talked with him and asked if i could sit in on his course. He thought it was a terrific idea, and said that i could be in his tutorial. i learned a lot while taking that course. i learned about university, myself, and literature. i know that i could go to university if i wanted to, now that i understand what they are all about.

Wondertree isn't just a sweet wishy washy thing. Some of us did a year's math curriculum in four months. Some of us taught ourselves to read. We could go back to school and understand it was a game and play it. People learn when they are enthusiastic and passionate. That is why natural learning and emerging curriculum is so important.

At the end of eight years of Wondertree i decided i wanted some solitude and some time on my own. For two years i explored and learned—no school, no Wondertree, completely following my rhythms. I didn't have many friends. At the time i often thought i wasn't doing anything. But looking back on it i realize that i learned so much. A lot of it was internal work, becoming familiar and comfortable with myself. I also had times of guilt, fear, and doubt. Almost everyone around me had been schooled. i felt different from everyone else, i saw things in such a different way. i worried that i'd made the wrong choice, why hadn't i followed the crowd? Then i realized, "Almost everyone follows the crowd. You have done something different, ilana. You have done something revolutionary that is very right for you. You trusted yourself. That is what is important."

Then Dad and a friend created Virtual High. The Wondertree model grew up. Now Virtual High is in a mansion and Wondertree Education Society runs out of it. There are three Wondertree centers, and we have our own computer network. Our biggest project is to create the sustainable village (for 100 families) that we as a family have wanted since the beginning. Wondertree is about community.

No matter where i go i will have with me the gifts of love, creativity, and playfulness. i will have Wondertree in my heart forever. i thank my parents for being real with me. i thank them for listening to me.

★

The Declaration of Learners' Rights and Responsibilities was written by a group of seven learners and a mentor. We are a part of Virtual High—a learning community that grew out of Wondertree.

DECLARATION OF LEARNERS' RIGHTS AND RESPONSIBILITIES

1. As a learner I have the right to allow my own experience and enthusiasm to guide my learning.

2. As a learner I have the right to choose and direct the nature and conditions of my learning experience. As a learner I am responsible for the results I create.

3. As a learner I have the right to perfect the skills to be a conscious, self-confident and resourceful individual.

4. As a learner I have the right to be held in respect. It is my responsibility to hold others in respect.

5. As a learner I have the right to a nurturing and supportive family and community. My family and community have the right and responsibility to be my primary resource.

6. As a learner I have the right and responsibility to enter into relationships based on mutual choice, collaborative effort, challenge and mutual gain.

7. As a learner I have the right to be exposed to a diverse array of ideas, experiences, environments, and possibilities. This exposure is the responsibility of myself, my parents and my mentors.

8. As a learner I have the right to evaluate my learning according to my own sensibilities. I have the right to request and the responsibility to include the evluations of my mentors.

9. As a learner I have the right to co-create decisions that involve and concern me.

10. As a learner I have the right and responsibility to openly consider and respect the ideas of others, whether or not I accept these ideas.

11. As a learner I have the right to enter a learning organization which offers spiritual, intellectual, emotional, and physical support, and operates in an open and inclusive manner.

12. As a learner I have the right of equal access to resources, information and funding.

This document was created by Serena Staples, Gregory Dean, ilana Cameron, David Muncaster, Jesse Blum, and Sarah Partridge, with the help of Brent Cameron and other Wondertree Affiliates.

22

Windsor House

Meghan Hughes and Jim Carrico

Jim Carrico was born in Kitimat in 1957. His two children, Ana Rose (12) and Ruby (8), have attended Windsor House since September 1994 and are thriving. With a degree in Vegetation Ecology, Jim has spent much of the last twenty years closely examining the effects of clearcut logging on coastal rainforests. Recent enthusiasms include developing non-linear interactive information systems on the Mac platform, electronic publishing (so we don't have to cut down trees for paper), and Meghan.

Meghan Hughes attended Windsor House for five years, and has been a core teacher there for the past six. She received a BA from Antioch College in Ohio and has a teacher's certificate from Simon Fraser University, British Columbia. She is an avid quilter, cat lover, non-coercive education advocate and facilitator of workshops on Windsor House and free schools.

Windsor House is unique in this collection, and very rare otherwise, in that it is a radical alternative school, modelled largely on Sudbury Valley School, and yet is entirely publicly funded. That the school's community has managed to maintain this status is a testament to their success, negotiating skills, and the strength of their parent group.

SITUATED ON A LOW RIDGE OVERLOOKING THE PORT OF NORTH Vancouver in British Columbia, Windsor House School seems at first glance like any other in the district. Constructed to house the Cloverly Elementary School, the building is a paragon of 1960s' institutional architecture. About a dozen classrooms lie astride a single two-story axis, with a gymnasium complex forming the bottom of an L, and a broad, flat field behind. Walking down the hallway on a weekend or an evening when the school is empty, one might glimpse a ghost of the way it was: classes filled with desks in rows, all eyes facing the teacher at the blackboard, every notebook open to the same page until a bell announces it's time to open another. But there's something very different going on around here these days.

A group of visitors were recently somewhat astounded to stumble into the midst of the Saxon invasion of Britain (circa AD 900)—children dressed in flowing robes and cardboard armor furiously defending the castle Camelot against newspaper-sword-toting attackers advancing and retreating in waves up and down the hall. On another day the same group may have seen a group of children hotly debating a new clean-up policy; or a plan to rename and re-purpose one of the classrooms; or whether or not there should be a new voting category, in addition to "in favor," "opposed," and "abstain," called "really don't care." Or perhaps they may arrive on a warm spring day to find nearly every student and staff member outside enjoying the sunshine. It's even possible that they may find a group of students in a classroom, attentive to a teacher at a blackboard, although the "teacher" may be a parent or one of the students. First-time visitors may be inclined to think that Windsor House is disorganized, but there are very strong underlying principles at work, and it is a form of organization that becomes apparent as soon as the usual preconceptions are put aside about what a school is and should be.

The philosophical bedrock on which Windsor House rests is non-coercive education, the belief that human beings will eagerly learn what they are interested in learning, and resent being forced to do, say, think, or learn anything that does not interest them. Complementing this is a strong sense that healthy development must take place in the context of a healthy community, and much effort has been made to create and maintain a micro-society in which parents, staff, and children participate equally. The vitality of the school depends heavily on the day-to-day involvement of parents and other adult members of the community (including former students), who provide a diversity of skills, interests, and enthusiasms, and a strong network of physical and emotional support. Among the few schools in British Columbia that have attempted to realize this philosophy, Windsor House is unique in that it lies entirely within the administrative bosom of the School Board and the Ministry of Education, and receives the same funding and pupil/staff ratio as any other public school.

The student population of Windsor House has been rising steadily for some time, with current enrollment hovering around ninety, from five to sixteen years old. Some of the parents bring their infant children to school with them, which further extends the continuum of age and developmental level. Because the students are free to move about the school as they please, the stratification by age that is a fixture of conventional education is entirely absent, and they naturally group around common interests and activities. Learning at Windsor House is sought out and initiated by the children. Structured classes are provided for those who ask for them, and although "unsolicited" classes may be offered by staff members or parents, no student is compelled to attend.

The community is particularly careful about subtle forms of coercion, typically of the form, "If you don't learn to —, then you'll never be able to —," which some parents may tend to apply if their child doesn't seem to be "choosing" to learn the basic academic skills at the same rate as kids their age in other schools. This is understandable given the depth of ingrown assumptions about education that most of us have been brought up with. By painful experience, however, this attitude has been seen to lead directly back to a formal curriculum, or at the very least the creation of hidden agendas that undermine the child's ability and desire to seek out his or her own path. The one thing that cannot be taught is self-knowledge: "What do I enjoy?" "What animates and interests and motivates me?" Ultimately no one can answer these questions but the individuals themselves and, in the absence of this knowledge, all the learning in the world is of little use. Non-coercive education is based on trust, and the conviction that people of all ages have a right to self-determination.

In harmony with this basic premise, the general forms and structures of the school are in a continual state of evolution. Aside from basic safety rules which are insisted upon by the School Board (and to a large extent by common sense), every aspect of the operation of Windsor House is up for discussion and democratic vote by the whole community on a one-person, one-vote basis. Even the basic philosophy and direction of the school is the subject of ongoing debate; thus, Windsor House has no constitution of "entrenched" principles, but always reflects the views and concerns of current community members, and has in fact undergone major shifts over the years. At one time all decisions at Windsor House were made by unanimous consensus, but this was seen to provide a loophole for a sort of tyranny of the most stubborn, and was eventually abandoned in favor of a two-thirds majority vote.

It is ironic that in a society that sees itself as democratic, it would be taken for granted that children should be raised under conditions of virtual dictatorship. Giving children an equal right to participate in setting the standards and guidelines by which they will live seems necessary if they are to mature into adults that are capable of participating in a genuine democracy. Windsor House is hardly without rules: there are plenty. The important thing is that anyone who dislikes a rule is free to gather support to change it.

Nor is Windsor House without conflicts: they happen literally every day. Every effort is made to resolve them in as creative and constructive a manner as possible. The current judicial system is based on a rotating committee of student volunteers, with one staff member, which meets two or three times a week to deal with complaints and infractions of standing resolutions. The accused are always given the opportunity to defend themselves, and consequences, if necessary, are set appropriately (e.g., mandatory separation for the rest of the day or week for fighting). The ultimate consequence is temporary or permanent exile from the community: there are probably very few schools at which the most dreaded punishment is not to be allowed to attend. But even this can't really be called punishment, it being ultimately a matter of freely choosing to participate in a community, or not, according to rules openly created and enforced by everyone.

In all of this, the structures that are created deal mainly with what children and adults cannot do; what they can do tends to be left open. Over a period of time, different uses have evolved for certain rooms; a library, of course, and an art room, a computer room, and so on; but also a room for just lounging around in, and another specifically dedicated to horseplay. Occasionally the whole school is involved in a single activity, most notably during the simulation games that have been held on a regular basis for many years. These are conceived of as on-going theater pieces using the entire building and grounds as a stage, for which there is no audience but the actors themselves. Participants are responsible for developing their own characters, and writing their own parts, and much time and preparation goes into sets, costumes, and collectively drafting scenarios for the plot. In some ways it replaces a traditional social studies class, but develops a much broader range of skills, and happens to be a lot more fun. This past year the game covered the Celtic culture from 200 BC up to the time of King Arthur. Previous games have dealt with ancient Greece and Egypt, West Coast natives, and even the Paleolithic Era.

Students frequently plan and carry out role-playing games on a smaller scale, or other self-organized activities. Recently a group of seven- to ten-year-olds passed a resolution to sell hot dogs and floats at lunch time. With the help of a staff member and a parent, the "Pig-Out Stand" has made an average profit of $50 per week, split evenly between the school and the student entrepreneurs. Some of the younger boys gained approval to begin digging a "mine" in an overgrown slope behind the school, and have been bagging for sale "natural soil," with half the proceeds to be donated to help the Pygmies save their rainforest homes. After about a week, one of the parents took a resolution to a school meeting that children refrain from digging in the roots of the nearby trees, drawing attention to the way our activities can affect our surroundings in unintended ways, and incidentally contributing to the hands-on democracy of Windsor House.

The spontaneous atmosphere belies the years of conscious effort and experimentation that have gone into the development of the culture of Windsor House. The school was founded in 1971 by Helen Hughes (who remains at the center of community) at her house on Windsor Street (hence the name) in North Vancouver. The school evolved out of a parent-participation preschool at which Helen had taught, but was specifically necessitated by the degree to which her daughter Meghan, then age eight, despised public school. The school began with an enrollment of 25 children aged five to eight, and was paid for largely by the day care that Helen provided before and after school. After four years of shoestring budgets and overcrowding, a group of parents successfully lobbied the School Board to finance the school as a special program within an existing elementary school.

The next fifteen years saw a slow process by which the school began to resemble more and more the rest of the school system, as one after another piece was introduced: 20 minutes per day of mandatory instruction led to folders of basic work to be completed each day, which led to using the mornings for schoolwork and afternoons for "fun" activities, which eventually led to structured classes and activities all day long. In 1989, a group of community members visited Sudbury Valley School, and our experiences led to an attempt to reverse this trend and return the school to its non-coercive roots. This initiative resulted in a near-fatal conflict that literally split the school in two. But by rediscovering its original philosophy, and recommitting itself to a non-coercive pedagogy, Windsor House has recovered and emerged much stronger. Three years ago the school moved to its present Cloverly site.

Sometimes referred to as a "school for the severely unique," Windsor House is definitely not resting on its laurels. Simply maintaining its existence within an occasionally hostile system requires constant vigilance and effort. Part of its longevity is attributable to the political activism of many parents, attending school board meetings *en masse* when necessary to counter any threat to the program. Last year a complaint filed by an unhappy parent led to the formation of an external review committee to assess the situation. The team toured the school, attended meetings and interviewed community members, and delivered a positive report, describing the school as "vibrant" and fulfilling a "critical need." The team went on to recommend that additional space and staff be made available to the school, that it be allowed a permanent home in its current facilities, and that the program be expanded to grade 12. Some of these requests have been partially met, others are pending, but there have been no guarantees, and nothing is being taken for granted. The only constant is change: children grow, and the community continues to evolve.

23

Liberating Education

Satish Kumar

Satish Kumar is a former Jain monk who is now the editor of the magazine, Resurgence, *the founder of the Small School, and the Director of Programs at Schumacher College, all in England. His autobiography,* No Destination, *is published by Green Books.*

Satish is an important figure in the Small School movement in Britain and in the ecology movement world-wide through Resurgence *and the Schumacher College. His gentle and thoughtful views on industrialization and economies of scale are critical in maintaining community-based patterns of living, and his observations on deschooling are of crucial importance.*

THERE ARE TWO ASPECTS OF EDUCATION WHICH REQUIRE URGENT attention: firstly, the relationship between the state and education; secondly, the size of our schools.

Politics is an arena of short-term strategies. Policies are proposed to win votes and influence elections. These policies are often conceived in the interest of the parties rather than society as a whole. Politics is put before children, teachers, and parents. In my view, education is too important to be left to the politicians. Therefore, I believe that the administration of education in any country ought to be taken completely out of the hands of the politicians and given to an independent body. This kind of independent administration already operates to a limited extent in the higher education sector in Europe and America. As a result, there is less direct interference by the governments in universities. There should be independent educational boards, run by people who are free of vested interest, who are respected for their integrity, wisdom and educational experience.

In all countries of the world we need to mount a campaign to liberate education from governmental control. But governments are not likely to give up voluntarily the enormous power and influence that they exercise. So, the parents, teachers, and citizens will have to demand this liberation in no uncertain terms.

The second point that I am concerned with is the size of schools. In a nutshell, most schools in the world are too large. I believe that the pupils, parents, and teachers are the paramount agents of education. Buildings, gymnasiums, swimming pools, visual aids, modern equipment, and everything else come second. Our schools, for too long, have been governed by the economies of scale. The rule of saving money has forced our schools to grow larger and larger. The casualties of this approach have been the school's relationships with parents and personal attention to pupils. This type of education is managed not by intimate understanding of all involved, but according to the rule book.

Schools have come to resemble factories, whereas they should be extensions of homes. Instead of a trusting and friendly environment, fear and suspicion permeate the atmosphere of our schools. Problems of discipline, vandalism, and truancy are the direct results of this giantism. The teaching staff of a large school do not even know each other well, much less the parents of their pupils. In a large school the pupils are like strangers. How many teachers have time to talk with their pupils informally and often? From my own experience I know that most teachers are too busy to spare time to answer their parents' spontaneous questions, particularly in secondary schools.

Moreover, beyond a certain size even the economy of scale does not apply, as there are new costs involved. For instance, administrative and bureaucratic costs increase greatly and millions are spent repairing the damage. Even more millions are spent on children who don't get on in large schools and must be sent to special schools. And how many other millions are spent on pupils who fall victim to gangsterism, drug abuse, and theft, ultimately ending up in prisons and hospitals as burdens on society? The cost of uncared-for and unfulfilled children leaving a school cannot be measured in pounds and dollars.

In my view, our deepest social problems stem from our obsession to save money and organize schools on the principle of the economies of scale. What is necessary is that school culture and home culture be made compatible; schools would then be truly extensions of homes, and there would come about a strong partnership between home and school. That cannot be if schools have to deal with thousands of pupils and parents. Schools must be made smaller, much smaller. Schools should be part of the neighborhood and community, within walking distance of the pupil's homes. Smallness is the road to educational plurality. Some schools may have educational excellence in a particular field. Some may have a farm attached. Others may find excellence through craft or science or the arts.

These questions cannot be raised easily in our present education system. So, in order to explore the crucial questions of human existence and the meaning of life we are going to have to reorganize our educational institutions on a human scale, and those institutions are going to have to be independent of the state. Although this is a huge task, I believe that it is possible to liberate education, and to turn it into one of the highest human endeavors. Let us begin to carry it out now.

It is not enough to criticize the system and leave it at that. It is better to light a candle than to curse the darkness. In 1982 a group of us established the Small School, in England, precisely to make education free from state interference and to bring ecological and spiritual concerns into the life of the school. At present there are 30 children in the Small School. Following this example, six other small schools have been founded in England, and one in France. It is no good waiting for the governments to change their policy. People have to take the matter of education into their own hands, by establishing constructive examples, and by vigorous campaigning.

Part Five — A Reading and Resource List

Books, Magazines, and Organizations for Deschooling

These listings are intended as starting points for investigation. It's a big list, and it's only a start. There is an amazing wealth of resources out there; my investigations continually leave me smiling at the number of answers people have for their lives. I have added brief annotations to the pieces that have been particularly helpful to me.

Deschooling Books

Avrich, Paul, *The Modern School Movement.* Princeton: Princeton University Press,1980.

Bakunin, Michael, *On Anarchism.* Ed., Trans. Sam Dolgoff. New York: Knopf, 1980.

Bandura, Albert, *Aggression: A Social Learning Analysis.* Eaglewood Cliffs: Prentice Hall, 1973.

Barclay, Harold, *People Without Government: An Anthropology of Anarchy.* Seattle: Left Bank, 1990.

Bettelheim, Bruno, *The Children of the Dream: Communal Child-Rearing and American Education.* New York: Macmillan, 1969.

Bookchin, Murray, *Remaking Society.* Montreal: Black Rose, 1989.

Bookchin, Murray, *The Ecology of Freedom: The Emergence and Dissolution of Hierarchy.* Palo Alto: Cheshire Books, 1982. The classic work outlining his social ecology; vital for understanding anarchism, ecology, and community in the late 20th century.

Cayley, David, *Ivan Illich in Conversation.* Don Mills: Anansi, 1992. An excellent and readable series of interviews, offering a clear view of Illich, one of the most important thinkers of our time.

Colfax, David and Micki, *Homeschooling For Excellence.* New York: Warner, 1988.

Dennison, George, *The Lives of Children*. Reading, MA: Addison Wesley, 1969. A wonderful story of an alternative school in New York.

Dewey, John, *Democracy and Education*. New York: Macmillan, 1916.

Freire, Paulo, *Education for Critical Consciouness*. New York: Continuum, 1973.

Freire, Paulo, *Pedagogy of the Oppressed*. New York: Herder and Herder, 1981. This is a classic, and critical for understanding deschooling ideas in the context of the "developing world" and adults.

Freire, Paulo, *The Politics of Education*. South Hadley, MA: Bergin and Garvey, 1985.

Gandhi, Mohandas K., *Gandhi's Autobiography*. Trans. Mahadev Desai. Washington D.C.: Public Affairs Press, 1948.

Gatto, John, *Dumbing Us Down*. Philadelphia, PA & Gabriola Island, BC: New Society Publishers, 1992. The man is brilliant; these essays are as moving as anything I've ever read.

Gatto, John, *The Exhausted School*. New York: Odysseus Group, 1993. A great series of essays from the first national speakout on the right to choice in education, organized by Gatto at Carnegie Hall.

Godwin, William, *An Enquiry Concerning Political Justice and Its Influence of General Virtue and Happiness*. Toronto: University of Toronto Press, 1926.

Goldman, Emma, *Living My Life*. New York: Dover, 1970. A deschooled heart and a great life.

Goodman, Paul, *Compulsory Miseducation*. New York: Horizon, 1969.

Greenberg, Dan, *Free At Last*. Framingham: SVS Press, 1973. A good account of Sudbury Valley School, perhaps North America's most famous free school.

Guterson, David, *Family Matters*. New York: Harcourt, Brace, Jovanovich, 1992. A cogent understanding of homeschooling by a clear writer and careful thinker.

Holt, John, *Escape from Childhood*. Boston: Holt Associates, 1974.

Holt, John, *Freedom and Beyond*. New York: Dell, 1972. This is one of Holt's last works, in which he carefully develops his conception of freedom.

Holt, John, *How Children Fail*. New York: Pitman, 1964.

Holt, John, *How Children Learn*. New York: Delacorte, 1967.

Holt, John, *Instead of Education*, Boston: Holt Associates, 1976. Perhaps my favorite Holt book, in which he describes his idea of a dignified environment for people to grow in.

Holt, John, *Never Too Late*. New York: Delacorte, 1984. A personal account of learning to play the cello in later life.

Holt, John, *Teach Your Own*. New York: Dell, 1981.

Illich, Ivan and Barry Sanders, *A.B.C.* New York: Vintage, 1988.

Illich, Ivan, *Celebration of Awareness: A Call for Institutional Revolution*, New York: Pantheon, 1971.

Illich, Ivan. *Deschooling Society*. New York: Harper, 1971. The most incisive and penetrating look at schools ever written. He is unrelenting and always unsettling, even after the twentieth read.

Illich, Ivan,et al., *Disabling Professions*. London: Marion Boyers,1977. With colleagues he expands the deschooling argument.

Illich, Ivan, *Medical Nemesis*. New York: Bantam, 1974. The same essential analysis, brilliantly applied. Schools are not making us smarter or more capable, hospitals are not making us healthier.

Illich, Ivan, *Towards a History of Needs*. Berkeley: Heyday, 1977.

Illich, Ivan, *Tools for Conviviality*. Berkeley: Heyday, 1973.

Kitzinger, Sheila, *Birth At Home*. New York: Oxford, 1980. I think deschooling and home birth are critically connected; this Kitzinger book makes the connections easy to see.

Kohl, Herb, *I Won't Learn From You!* New York: New Press, 1991.

Kozol, Jonathon, *Alternative Schools*. New York: Continuum, 1982.

Kozol, Jonathon, *Death at an Early Age*. Boston: Houghton Mifflin, 1970.

Kozol, Jonathon, *Free Schools*. Boston: Houghton Mifflin, 1972. A little dated, but his politics and vibrancy are always a joy as he describes the state of free schools in America in the late sixties/early seventies.

Kozol, Jonathon, *Savage Inequalities*. New York: Crown, 1991.

Kropotkin, Peter, *Mutual Aid: A Factor of Evolution*. Montreal: Black Rose, 1986. One of the great anarchist texts. The implications of his work for deschooling are staggering.

Leue, Mary, ed., *Challenging the Giant, Volumes I and II*. Albany: Down-to Earth,1992. A collection of essays from *Skolay* magazine and the Albany Free School, edited by a truly remarkable personality.

Llewellyn, Grace, *Real Lives*. Eugene: Lowry House, 1992.

Llewellyn, Grace, *The Teenage Liberation Handbook*. Eugene: Lowry House, 1991. A brilliant, readable and useful guide to unschooling for teenagers.

McKight, John, *The Careless Society*. New York: Basic Books, 1995. Maybe the best book on community I have read.

Miller, Alice, *For Your Own Good: Hidden Cruelty in Child-Rearing and the Roots of Violence*. New York: Farrar Straus, Giroux, 1984.

Miller, Alice, *Prisoners of Childhood: How Narcissistic Parents Form and Deform the Emotional Lives of Their Gifted Children*. New York: Basic Books, 1981.

Mintz, Jerry, ed., *The Handbook of Alternative Education*. 1994. A massive compendium of alternative education resources in North America. Can be ordered through AERO (see below, Networks and

Associations).

Montagu, Ashley, *Learning Non-Aggression: The Experience of Non-Literate Societies*. New York: Oxford University Press, 1978.

Neill, Alexander S., *Summerhill: A Radical Approach To Child Rearing*. New York: Hart, 1960. Still the most important writing on free schools around.

Neill, Alexander S., *Freedom Not Licence*. New York: Hart, 1966.

Pederson, Anne, and Peggy O'Mara, eds., *Schooling At Home*. Santa Fe: John Muir, 1990.

Reed, Donn, *The Home School Source Book*. Brook Farm Books, 1991.

Schumacher, E.F., *Small is Beautiful*. London: Blond and Briggs, 1973.

Sheffer, Susannah, *A Life Worth Living: Selected Letters of John Holt*. Boston: Holt Associates, 1990.

Shor, Ira, *A Pedagogy for Liberation*. South Hadley, MA: Bergin and Garvey, 1980.

Shor, Ira, ed., *Freire for the Classroom*. Portmouth: Boynton Cook, 1987.

Smith, Michael, *The Libertarians and Education*. London: Allen and Unwin, 1983. The best overview of the history of deschooling from William Godwin on.

Spring, Joel, *A Primer of Libertarian Education*. Montreal: Black Rose, 1975.

Wallace, Nancy, *Child's Work: Taking Children's Choices Seriously*. Boston, Holt Associates, 1990.

Ward, Colin, *The Child in the City*. London: Bedford Square,1976.

Wiener, Leo, Trans., *Tolstoy on Education*. Chicago: University of Chicago Press, 1967. A clear view of an honest mind addressing education with no fears.

Woodcock, George, *Anarchism and Anarchists*. Kingston: Quarry Press, 1992.

Deschooling Readings in Music
(compiled and annotated by Mark Douglas)

Ben-Tovim, Atarah and Douglas Boyd, *The Right Instrument for Your Child*. London: V. Gollancz, 1985. Challenges many assumptions regarding the best instrument to learn on. The authors suggest that an instrument can be a part of any person's life given two conditions: you choose the right instrument and you start at an appropriate time.

Casals, Pablo, *Joys and Sorrows*. New York: Simon and Schuster, 1970. An inspiring testament to the connections between living one's life and the world of music, told by a master musician and wise elder.

Chase, Mildred P., *Just Being at the Piano*. Berkeley: Creative Arts Book Company, 1985. Full of sensitive consideration and advice for parents, teachers and students of all ages. Worth reading every year.

Holt, John, *Never Too Late*. New York: Delacorte, 1978. Particularly valuable in this context as it describes the process of an adult learning to play a challenging instrument late in life.

Ristad, Eloise, *Soprano on Her Head*. Moab, Utah: Real People Press, 1987. Fascinating perspective and useful ideas on how to reconsider yourself and how you make music.

Sudnow, David, *Ways of the Hand*. Boston: Harvard University Press, 1978. Poetic and abstract. May be hard to take for some, may yield *satori* for others.

Magazines and Periodicals

The Drinking Gourd
   PO Box 2557, Redmond, WA 98073
   See Chapter 11: Dinosaur Homeschool.

Growing Without Schooling
   Holt Associates, 2269 Massachusetts Ave., Cambridge, MA 02140
   Contains many letters and articles demonstrating the legitimacy of a wide variety of experiences in regard to music education. See also Chapter 13: Doing Something Very Different.

Hip Mama
   P.O. Box 9097, Oakland, CA 94613
   A great new publication by single mothers from Oakland. Funny, smart and yup, hip.

Home Education Press
   PO Box 1083, Tonasket, WA 98855

The Journal of Family Life
   72 Phillip St., Albany, NY 12202
   Put out by the Albany Free School; see Chapter 19: A History of the Albany Free School.

Kids Lib News
   Box 28, Naalehu, HI 96772

Lib Ed
   Phoenix House, 170 Wells Rd., Bristol, UK B34 2AG

Natural Life
   RR#1, St. George, ON N0E 1N0 or
   P.O. Box 60, Lewiston, NY 14092-0060

New Moon
   PO Box 3587, Duluth, MN 55803-3587

Rethinking Schools
   1001 E Keefe Ave., Milwaukee, WI 53212

Self-Schoolers Network News
  RFD #1 Box 452, Lisbon Falls, ME 04252
Skipping Stones
  PO Box 3939, Eugene, OR 97403-0939 Tel: 503-342-4956
  Popular among homelearners with a multicultural focus.
SKOLE
  72 Phillip St., Albany, NY 12202-1789
  Published by the Albany Free School.
A Voice for Children
  7 Casa del Oro Court, Sante Fe, NM 87505

Networks and Associations

Alliance for Parental Involvement in Education (AllPIE)
  PO Box 59, East Chatham, NY 12060-0059
  Tel: 518-392-6900 allpiesr@aol.com
  See Chapter 17: AllPIE: A Learning Network.
Alternative Education Resource Organization (AERO)
  417 Roslyn Rd., Roslyn Heights, NY 11577
  Run by Jerry Mintz. Covers all kinds of alternative education from all
  over North America.
Alternative Education Resource Group
  39 William St., Hawthorne, Melbourne, Victoria 3122, AUSTRALIA
Association for Experiential Learning
  28885 Aurora Ave. #28, Boulder, CO 80303-2252
The Boiling Kettle
  P.O. Box 479, Wolfville, NS B0P 1X0
  Heidi Priesnitz's mail-order business (see Chapter 16).
Canadian Alliance of Homeschoolers
  Box 684, Stn. P., Toronto, ON M5S 2Y4
Center for Living Democracy
  RR #1, Black Fox Rd., Brattleboro, VT 05301
Clonlara School Home Based Education Program
  1289 Jewett, Ann Arbor, MI 48104
Educational Futures Project
  PO Box 2977, Sacramento, CA 95812
Holt Associates / John Holt's Book and Music Store
  2269 Massachusetts Ave., Cambridge, MA 02140
  See Chapter 13: Doing Something Very Different.

Human Scale Education
    96 Carlingcott, Nr. Bath, England, UK BA2 8AW
    See Chapter 23: Liberating Education.
The Love and Rage Community Society
    1450 Venables, Vancouver, BC V5L 2G1
    The learning center at which Matt Hern works.
Learning Unlimited Network of Oregon (LUNO)
    31960 SE Chin St., Boring, OR 97009
National Association of Alternative Community Schools
    PO Box 15035, Sante Fe, NM 87506
    A good collection of alternative schools with lots of interesting connections.
National Homeschool Organization / USA
    PO Box 157290, Cincinatti, OH 45215-7290
The New Zealand Home Schooling Association
    5 Thanet Ave., Mt. Albert, Auckland, NEW ZEALAND
The Odysseus Group
    295 8th St. W. #3, New York, NY 10009
    John Taylor Gatto's group.
Puerto Rico Homeschooling Association
    503 Barbe St., Santurce, 00912 PUERTO RICO
Separation of School and State Alliance
    4578 N First #310, Fresno, CA 93726
Sudbury Valley School Press
    2 Winch St., Framingham, MA 01710
    See Chapter 20: A School for Today.
TRANET
    PO Box 567, Rangeley, ME 04970
    I just found these folks, and they look great. They publish pamphlets and much else around a wide variety of community-based issues.
Windsor House
    440 Hendry Avenue, North Vancouver, B.C. V7L 4C5 CANADA
    Tel: 604-985-7315
    See Chapter 22: Windsor House.
Wondertree Education Society and Wondertree Homelearners Network
    1810 W. 16th, Vancouver, BC V6J 2M2 CANADA
    See Chapter 21: A Wonder Story Told by a Young Tree.